I0489829

PICTURE BOOK OF
SEASIDE
SERENITY

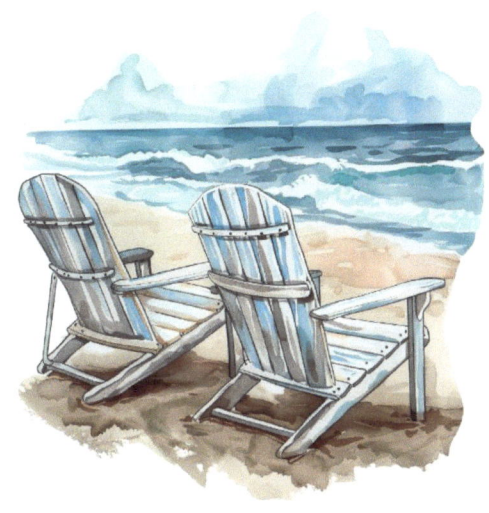

...By...

Ella Caldwell

Copyright © 2024. All rights reserved.

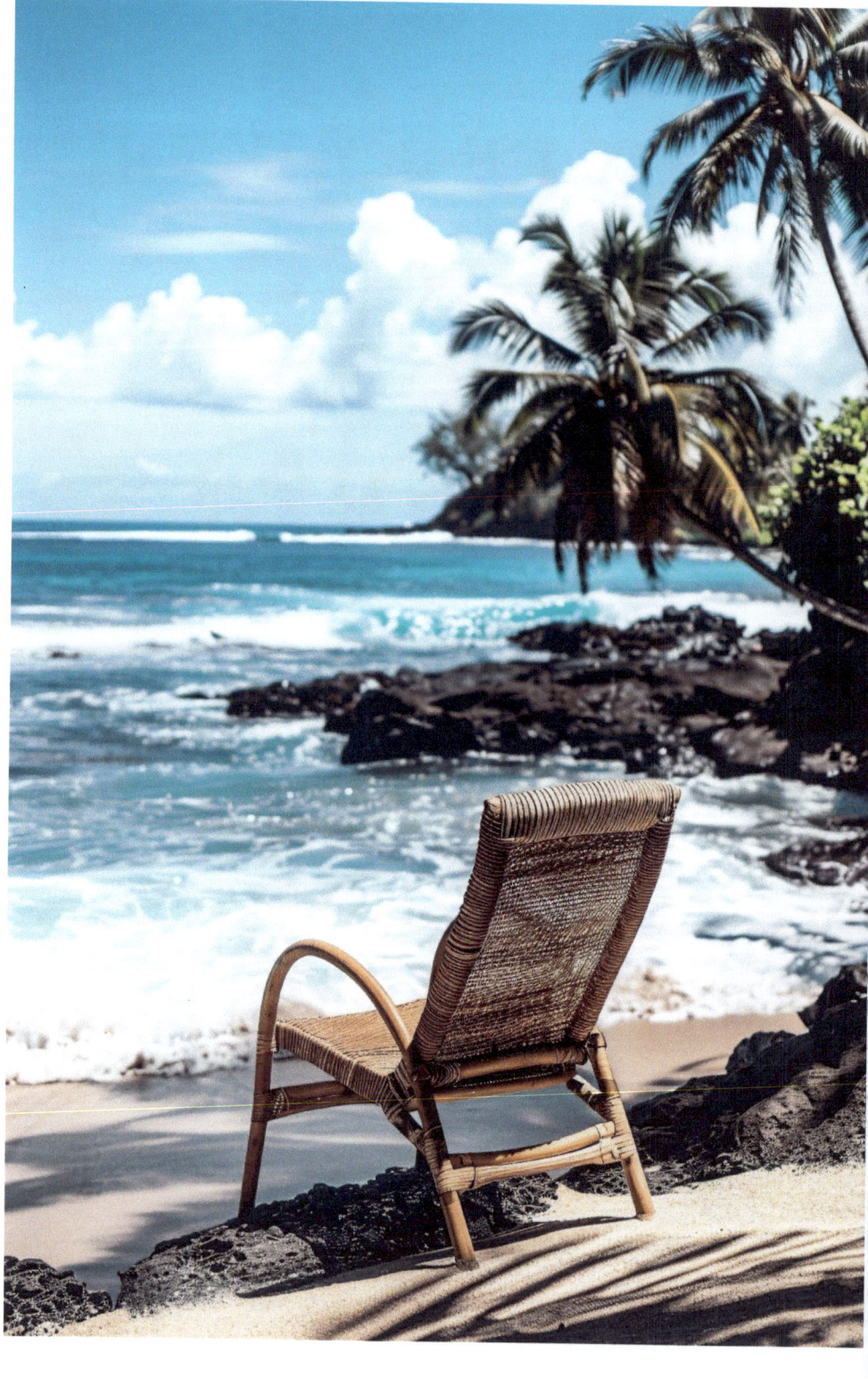

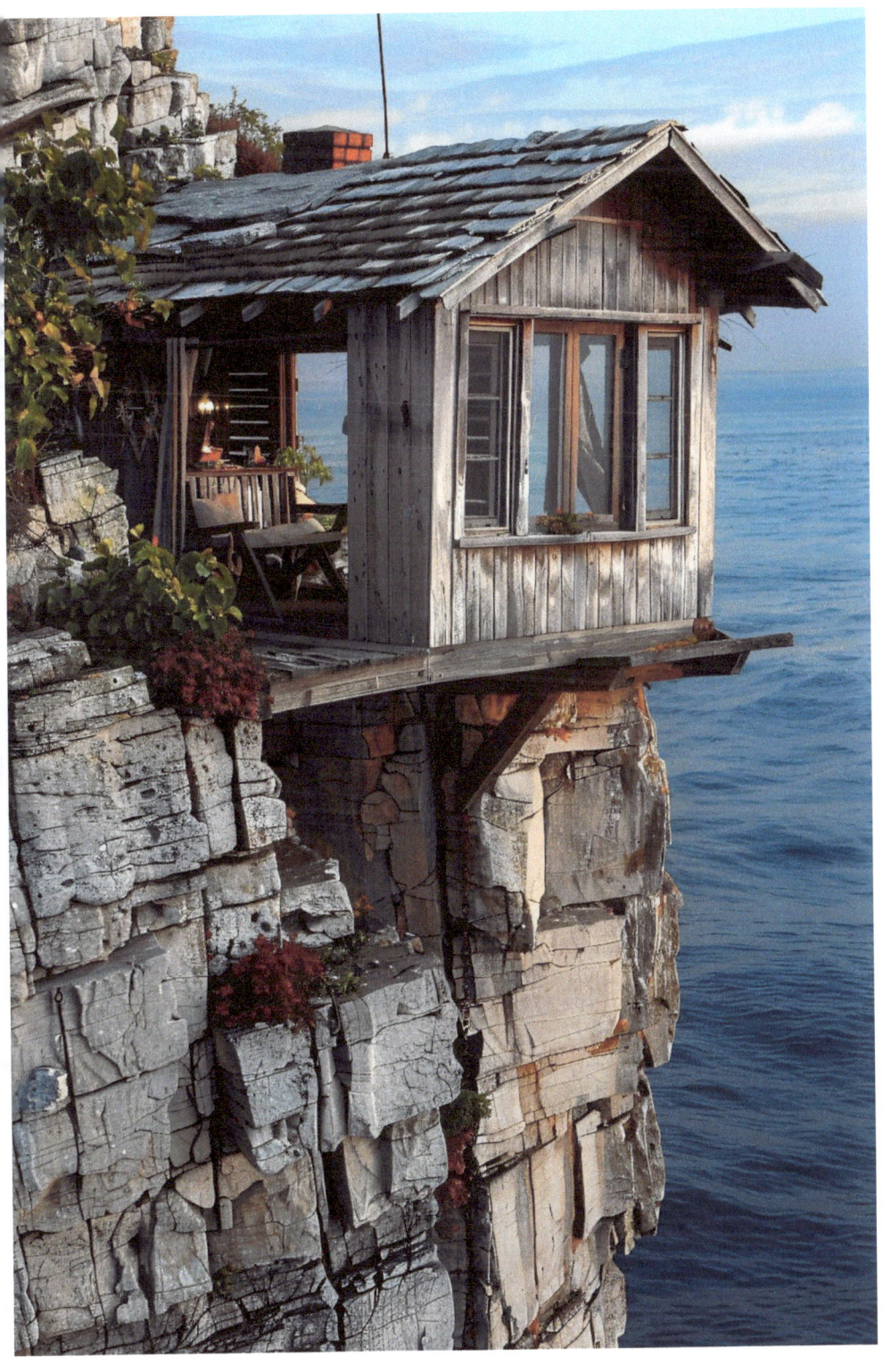

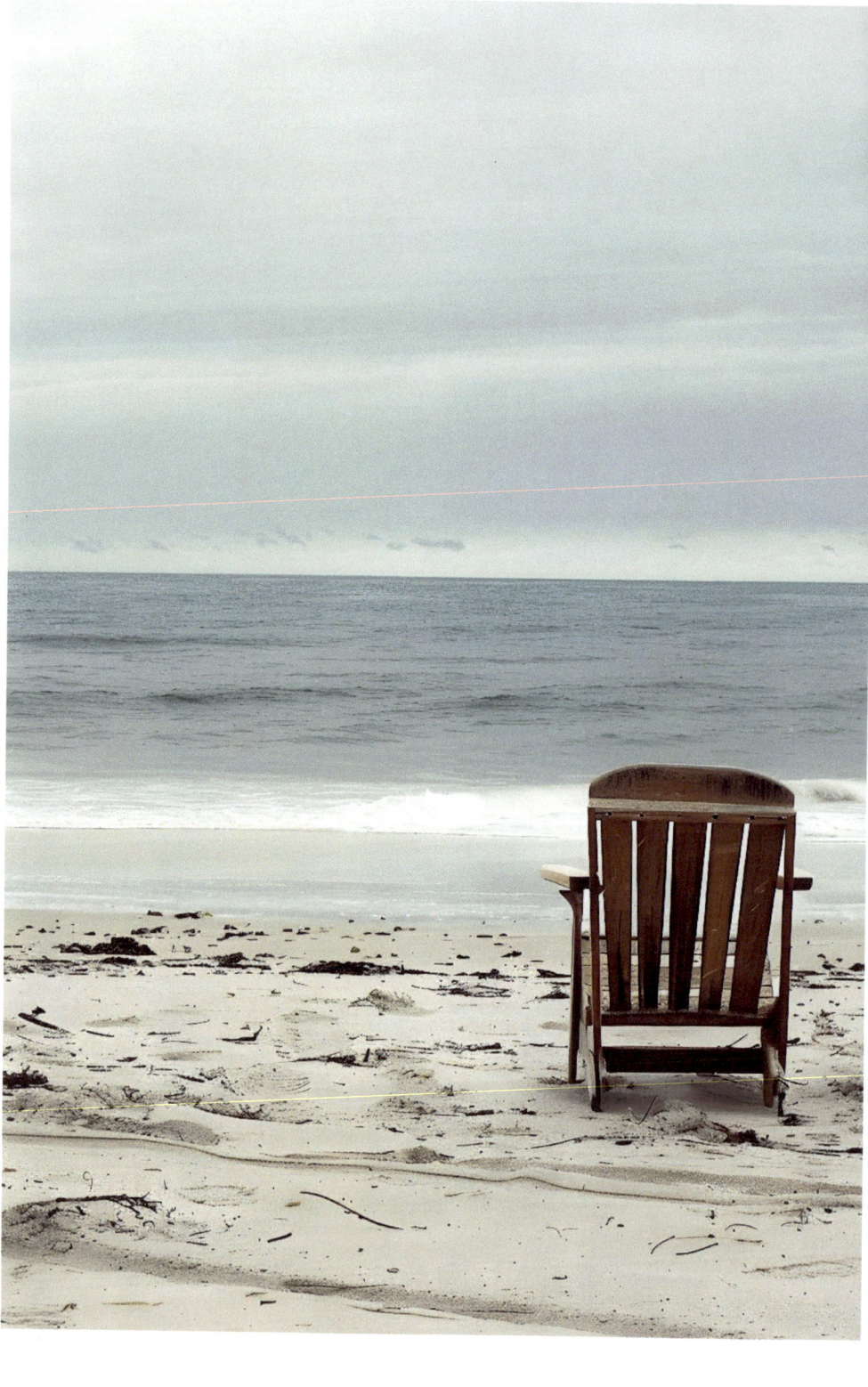

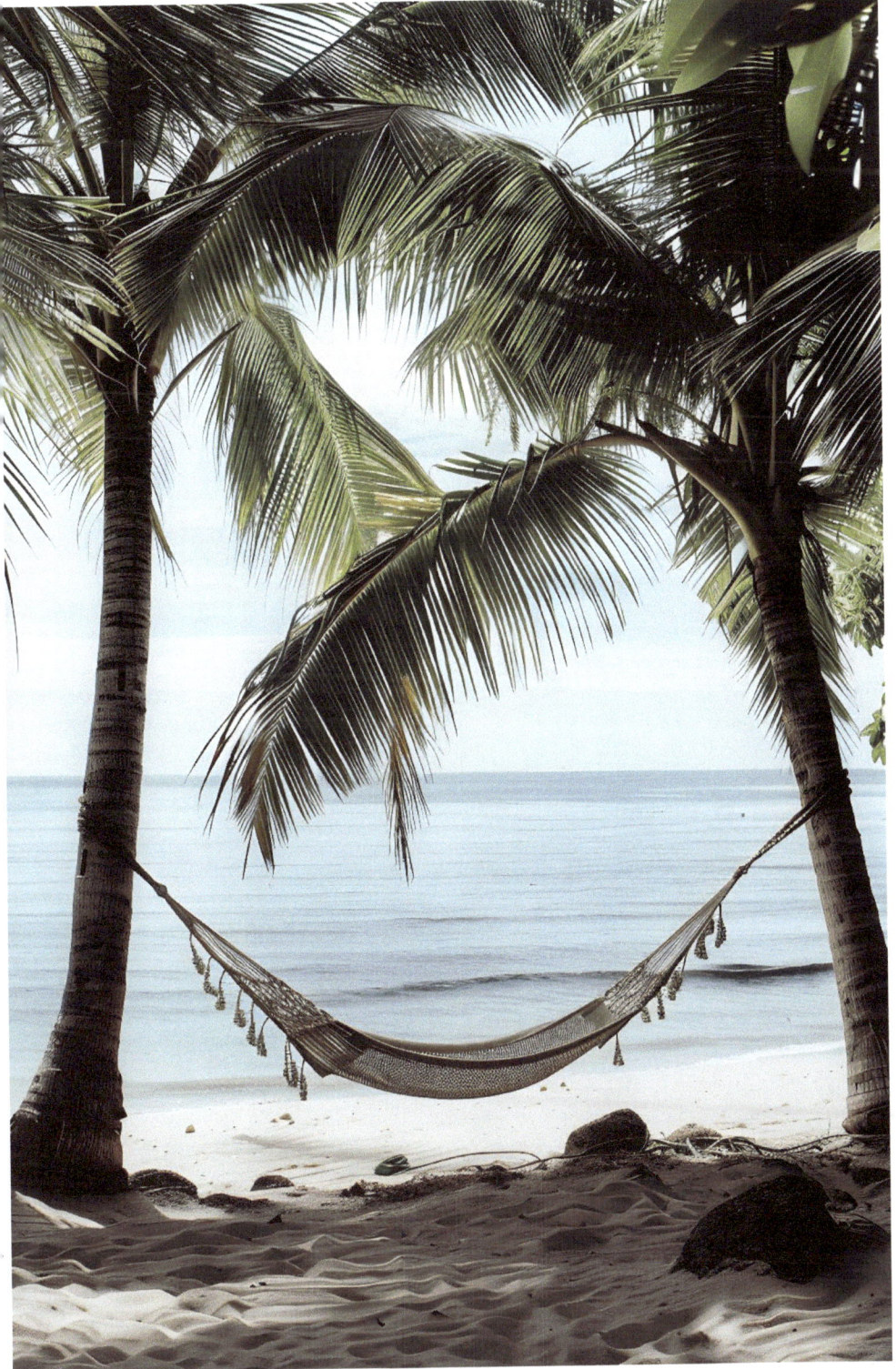

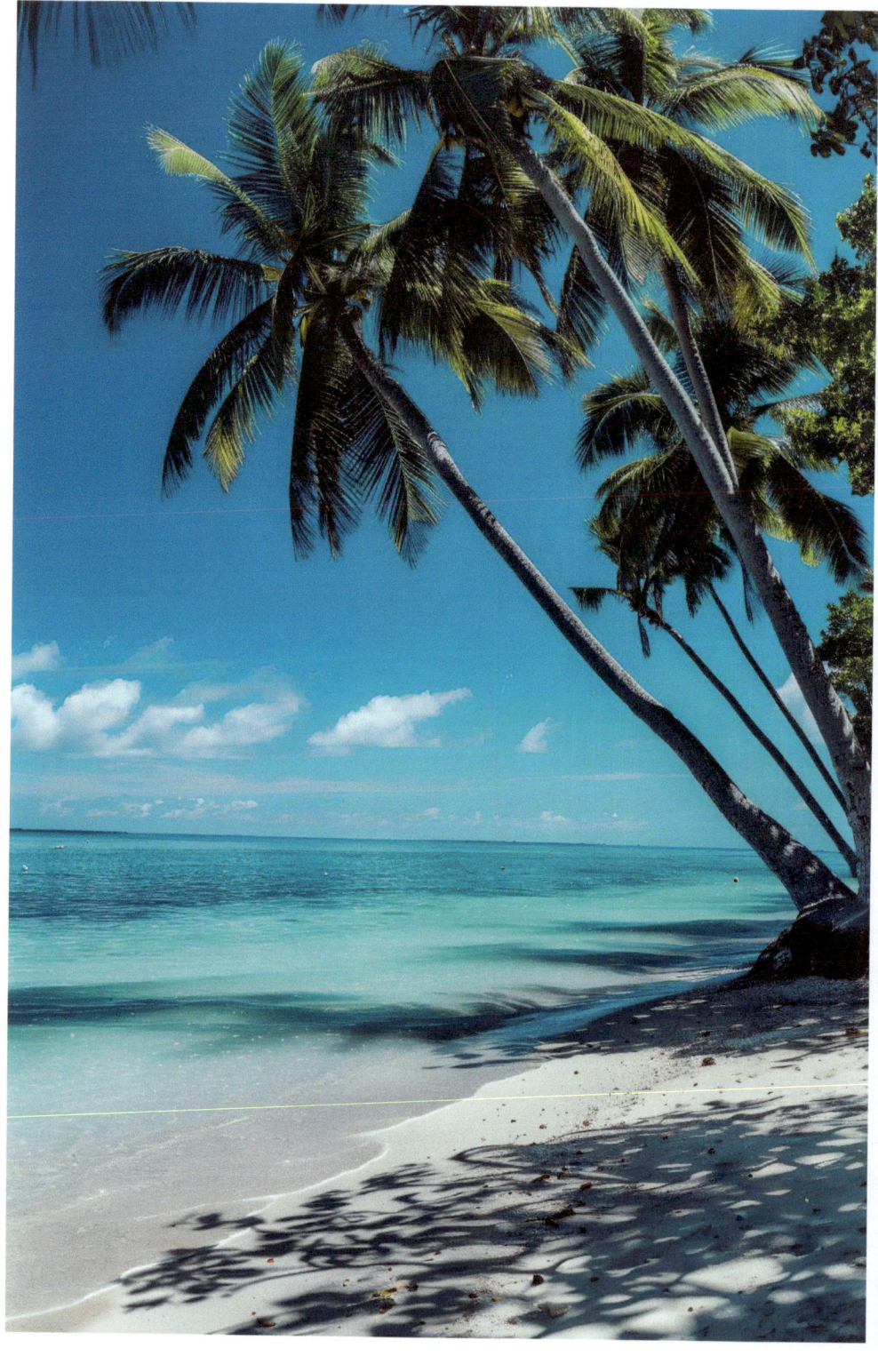

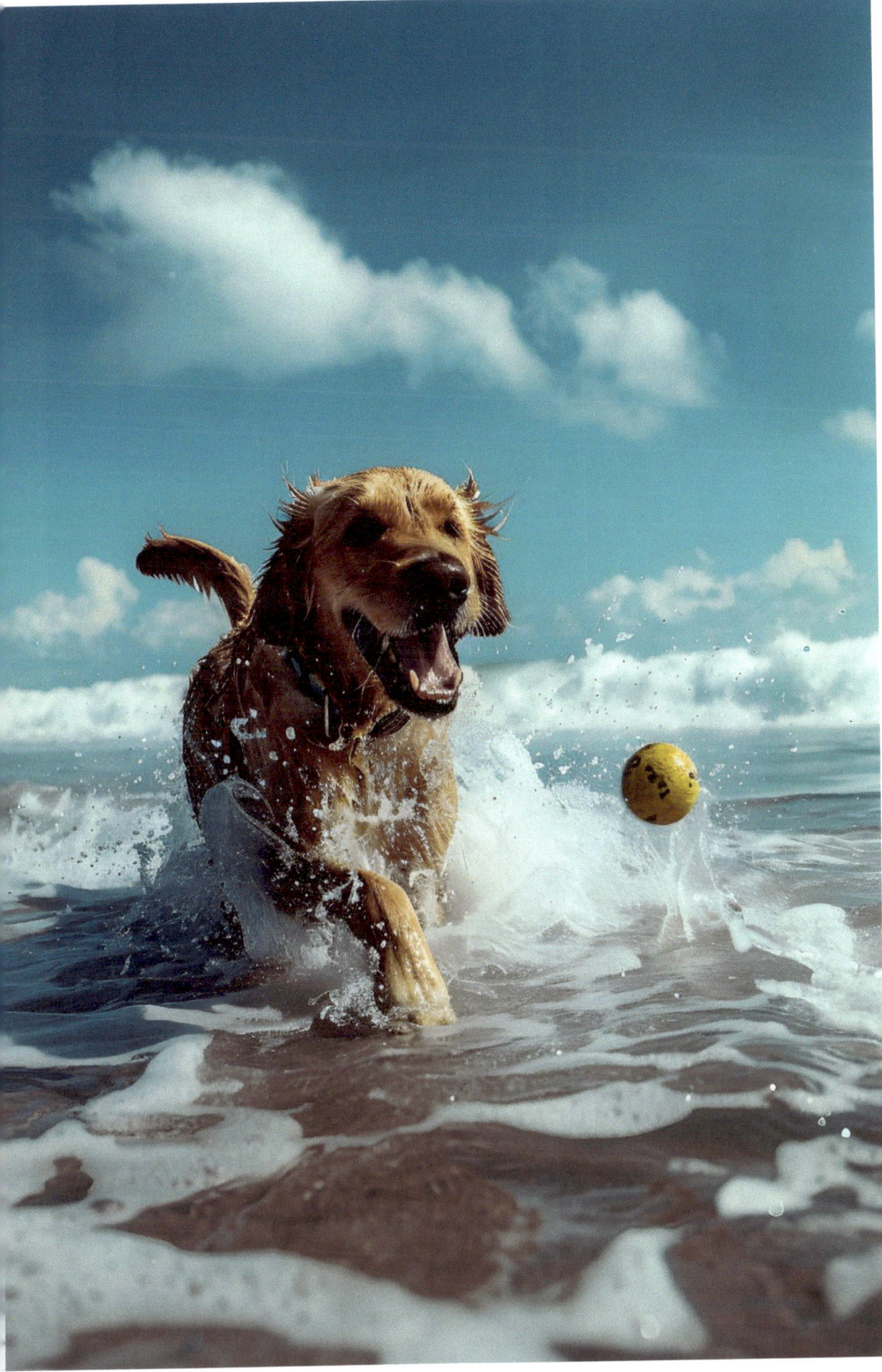

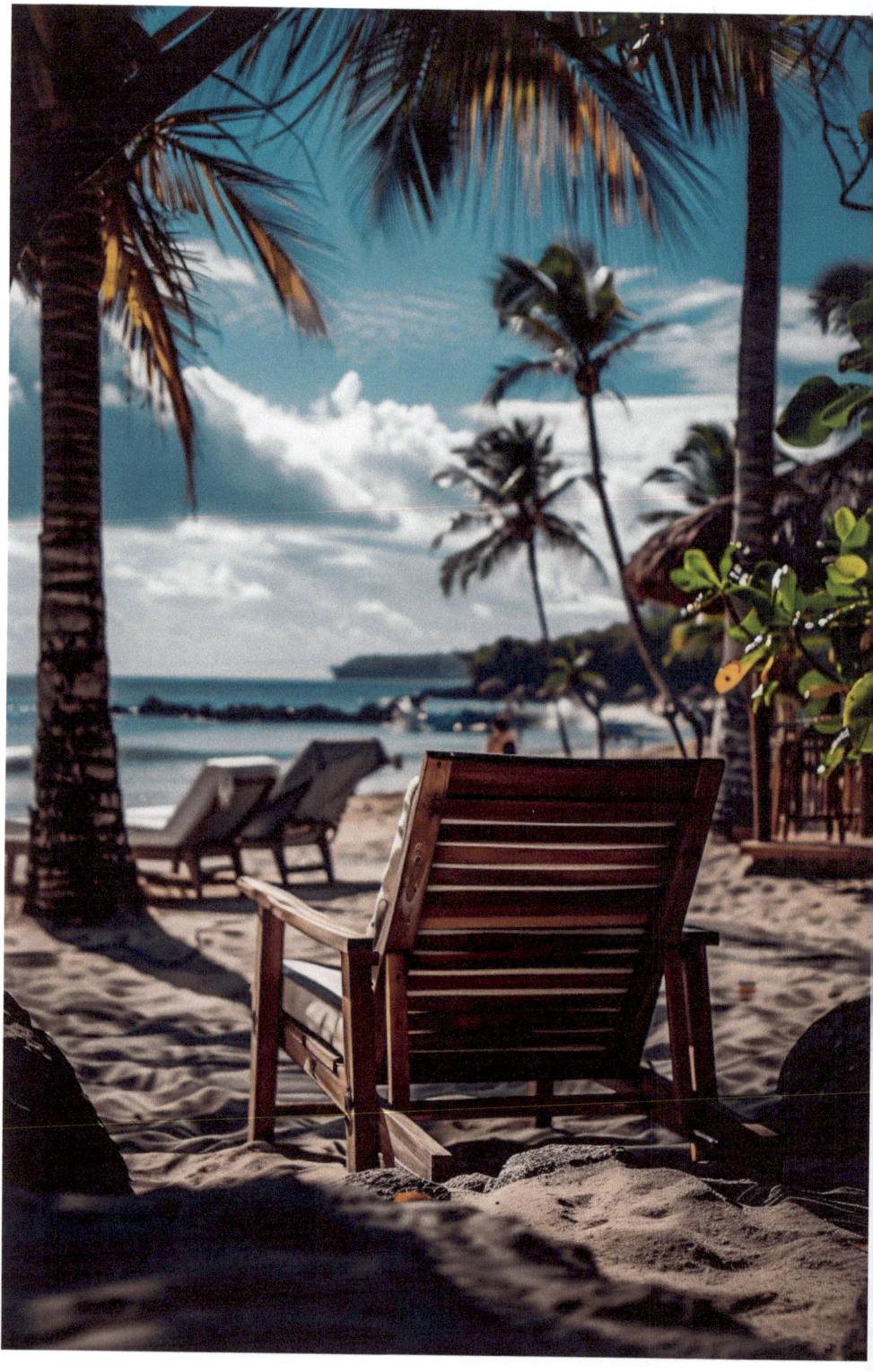

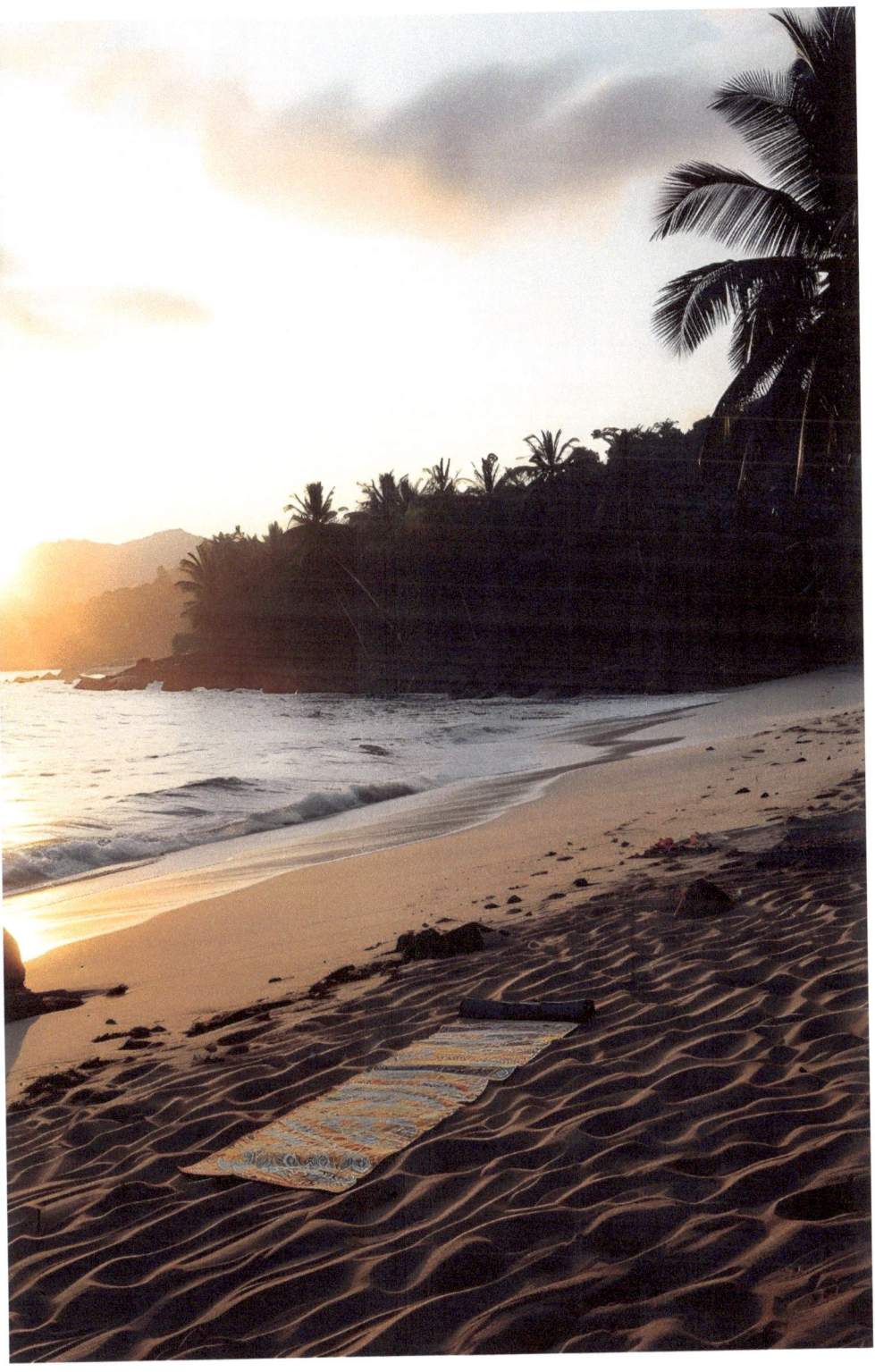

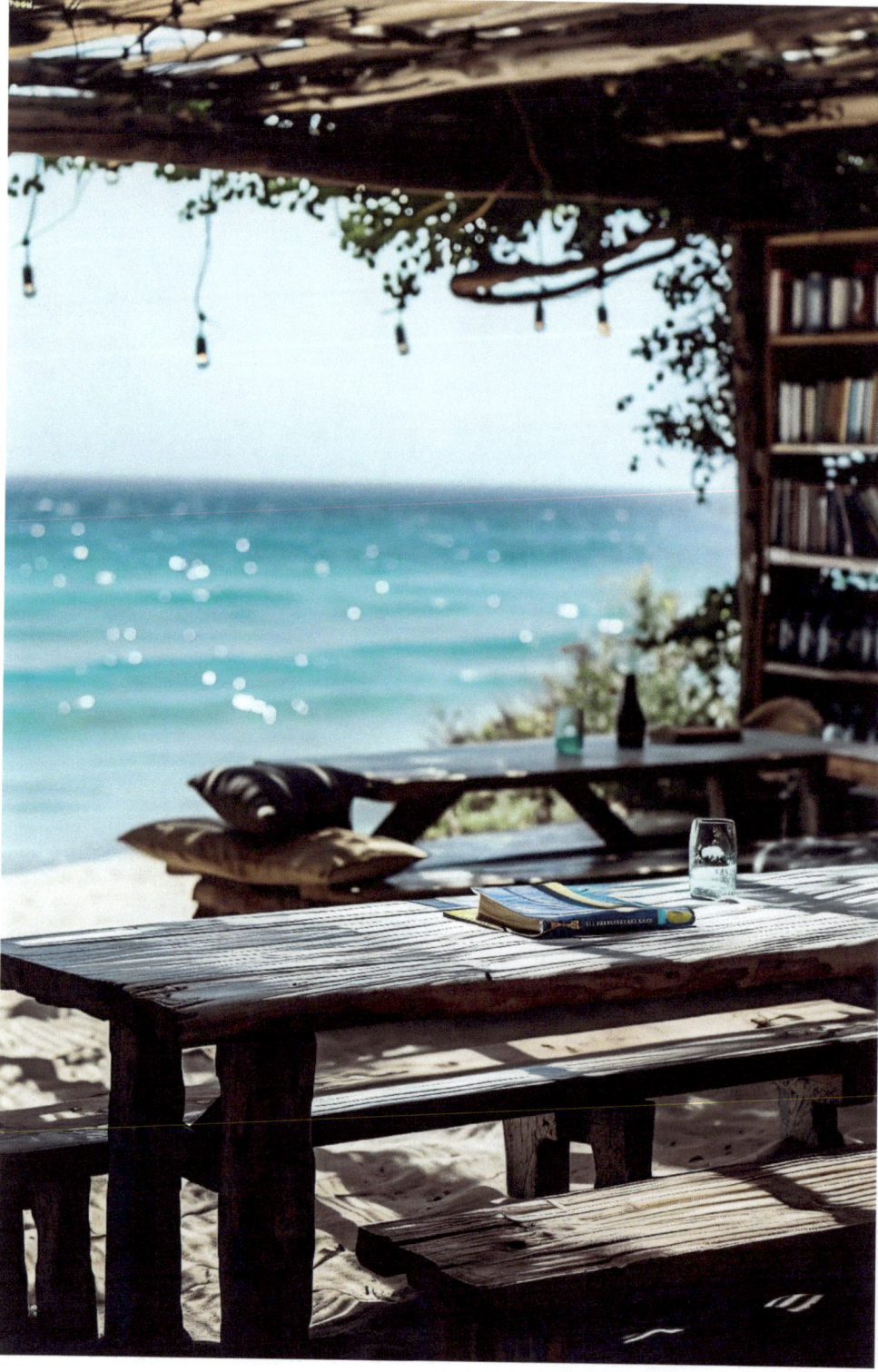

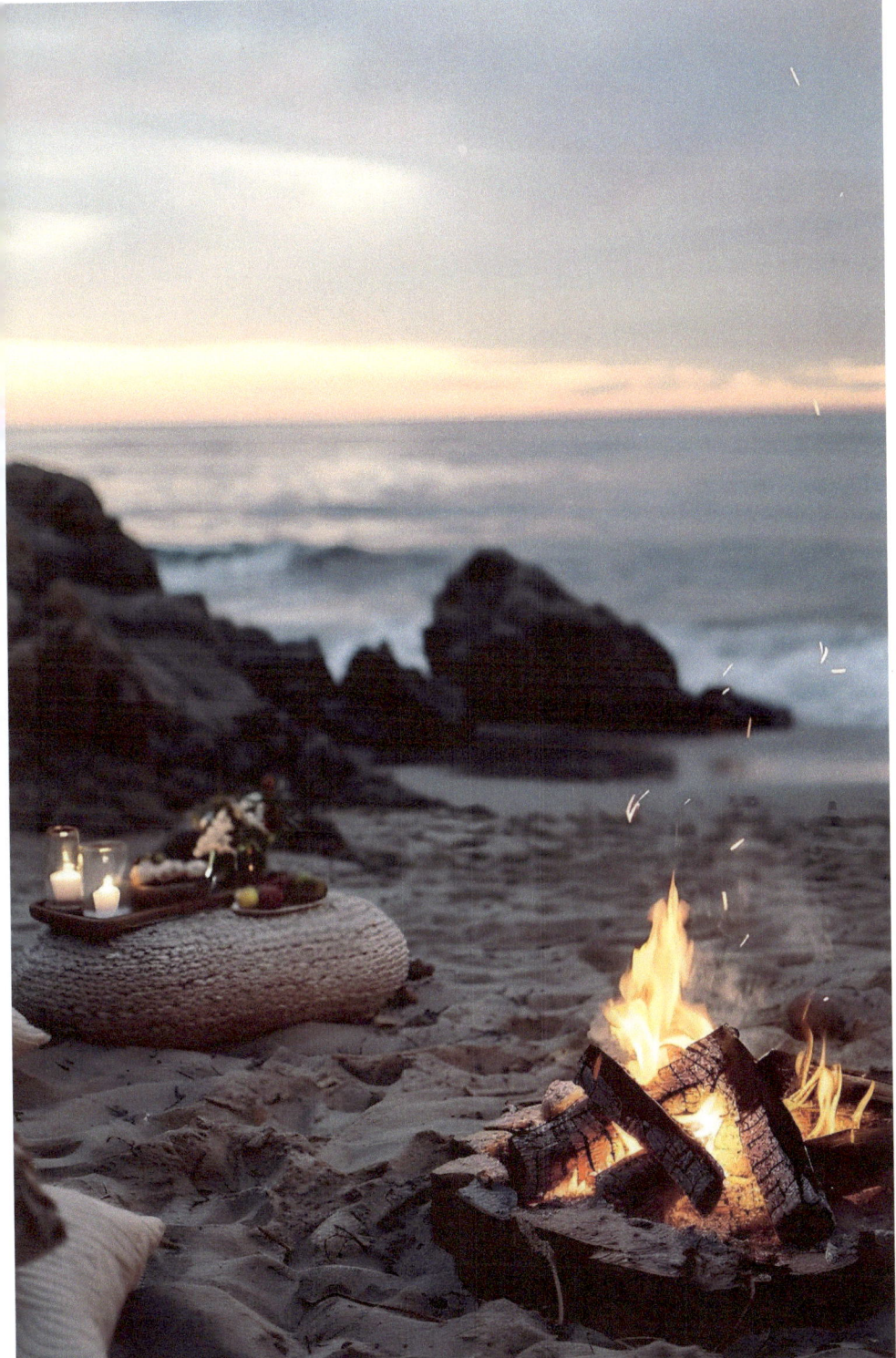

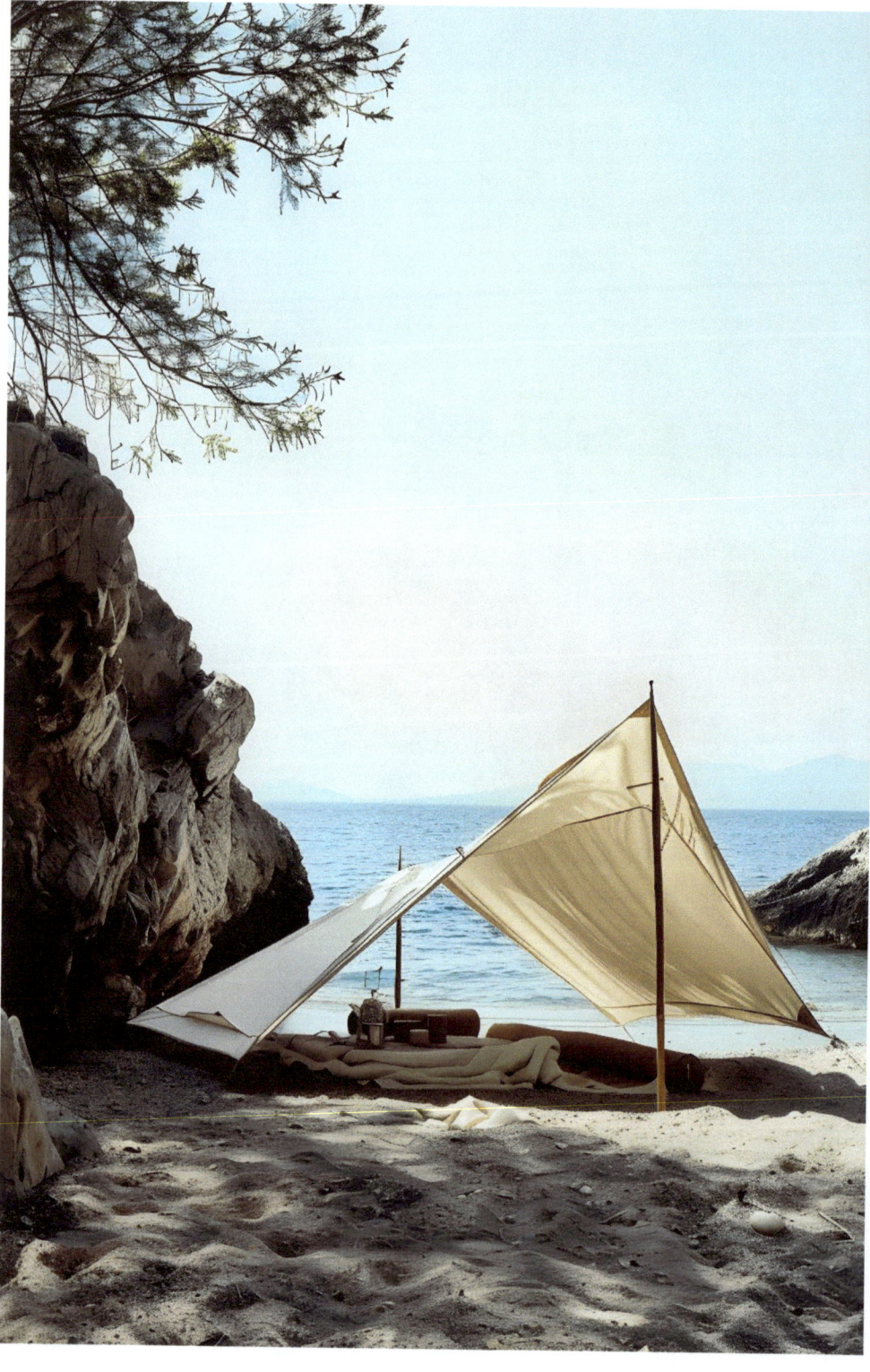

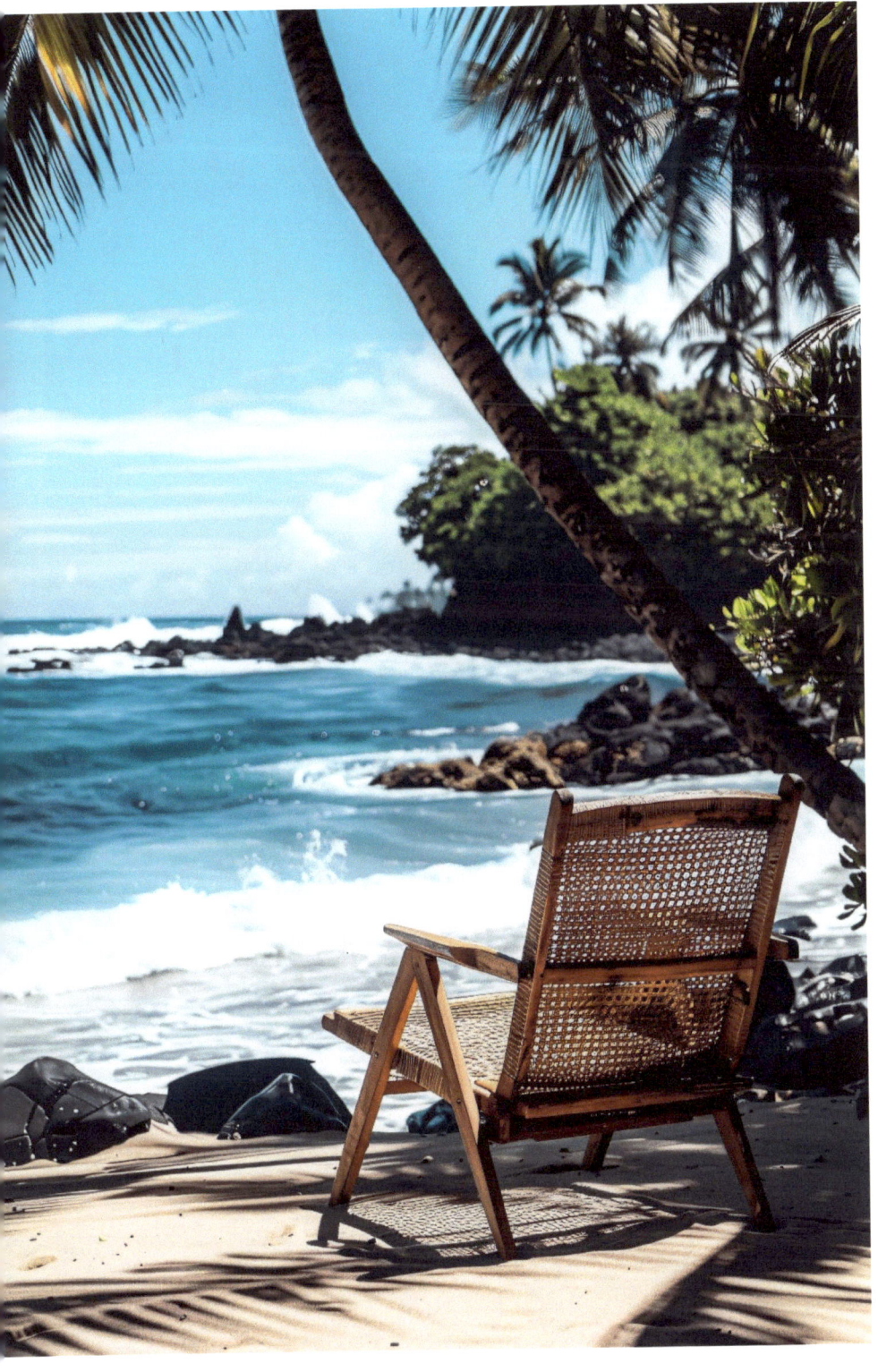

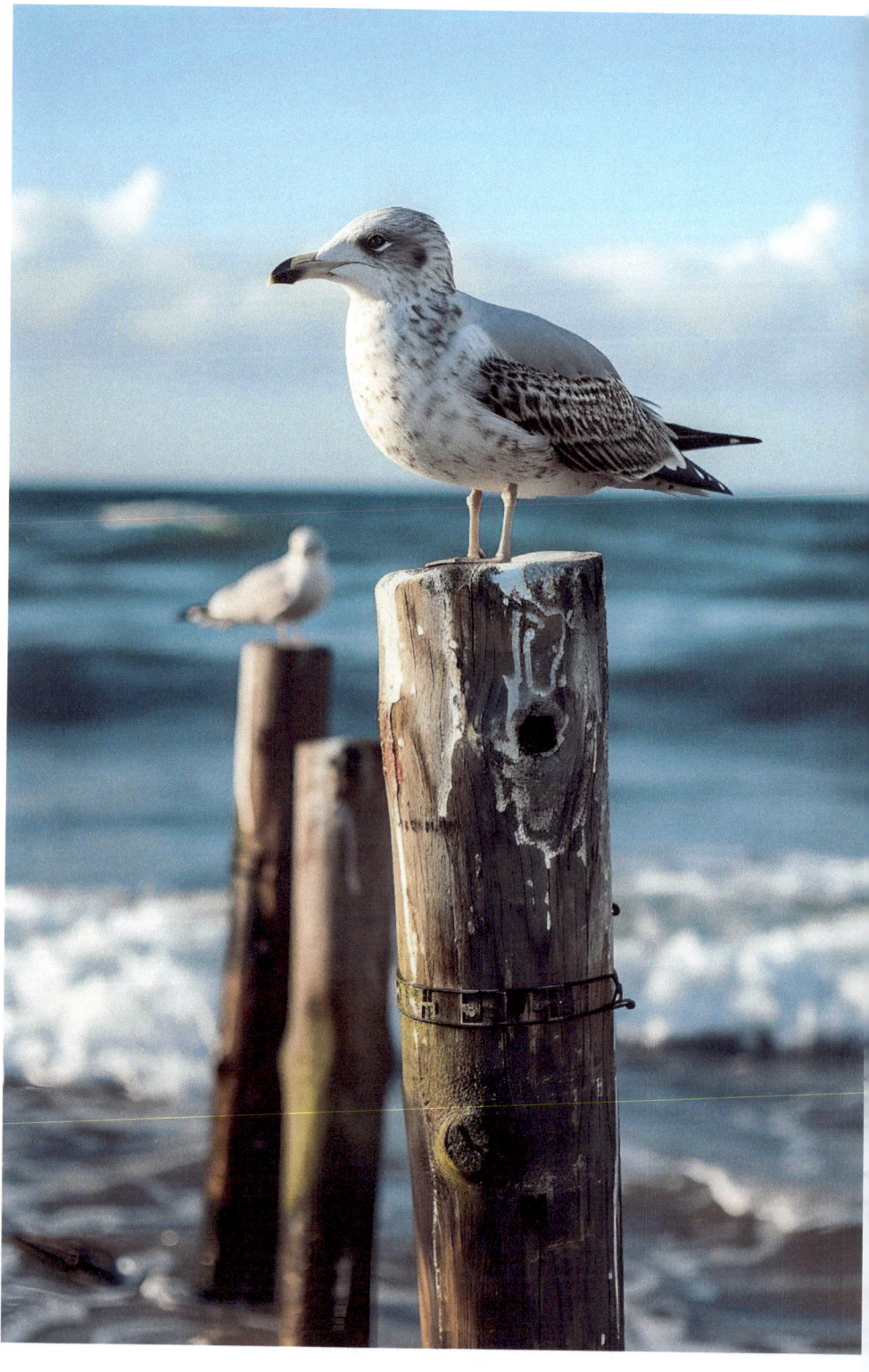

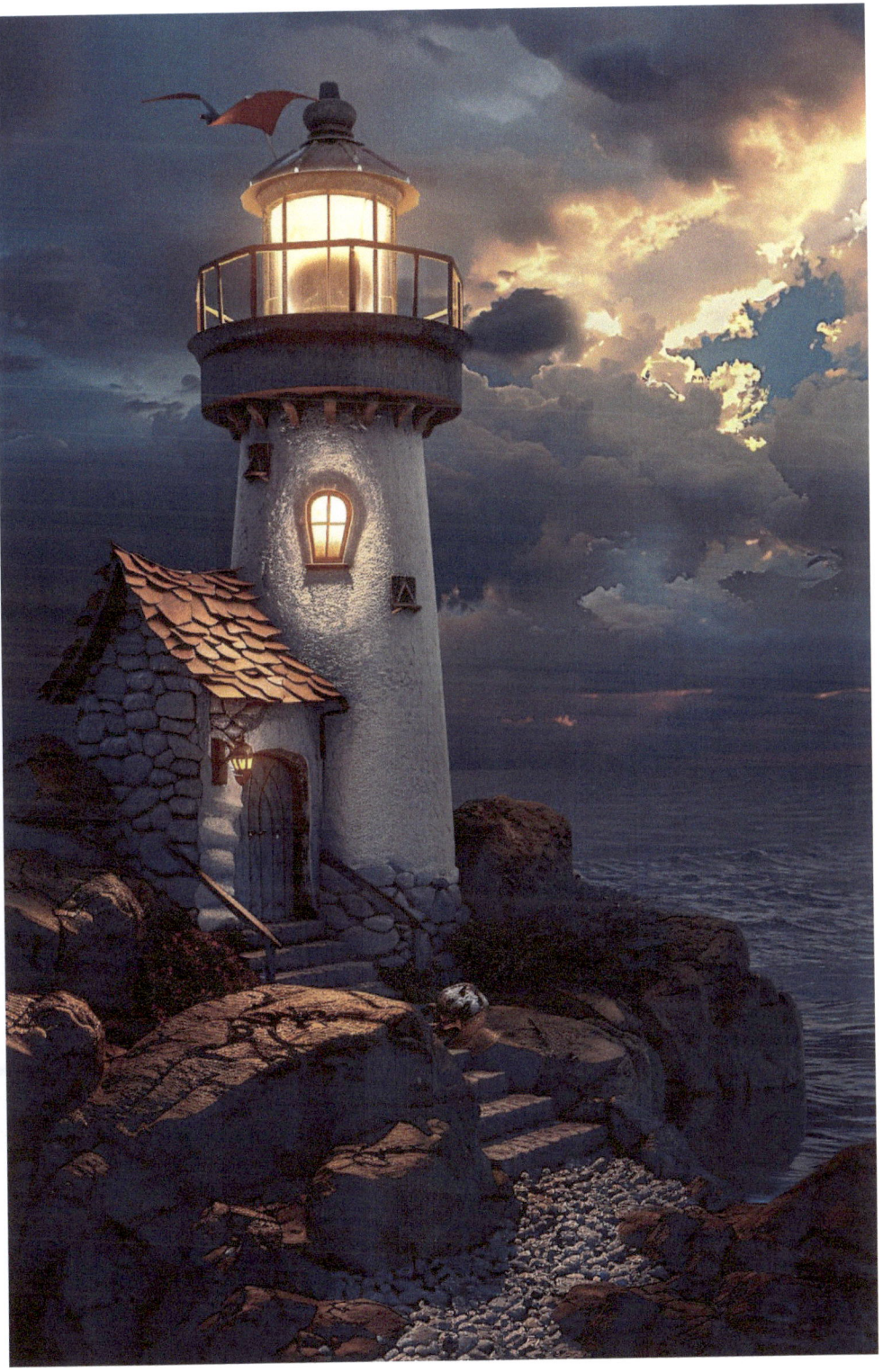

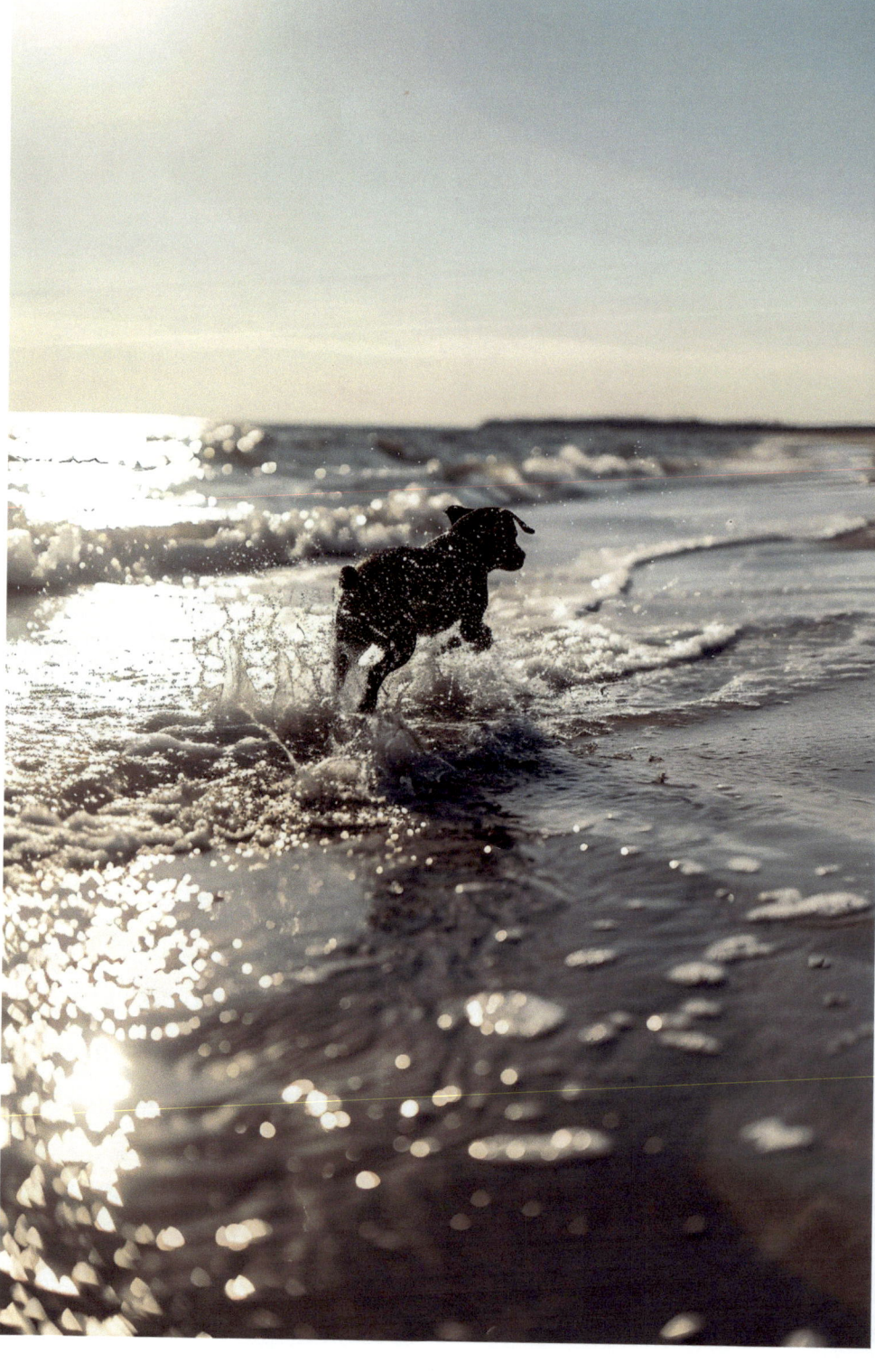

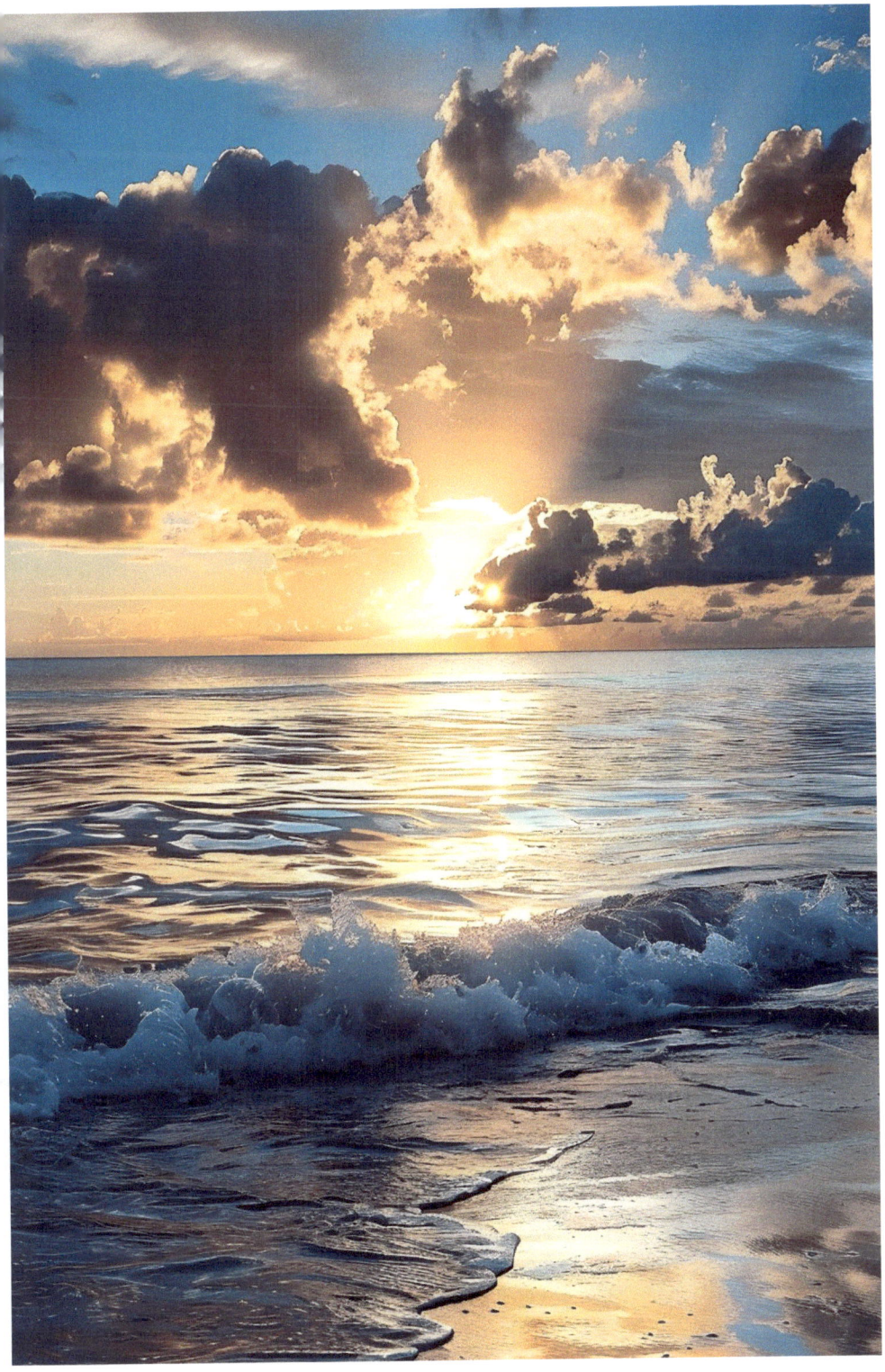

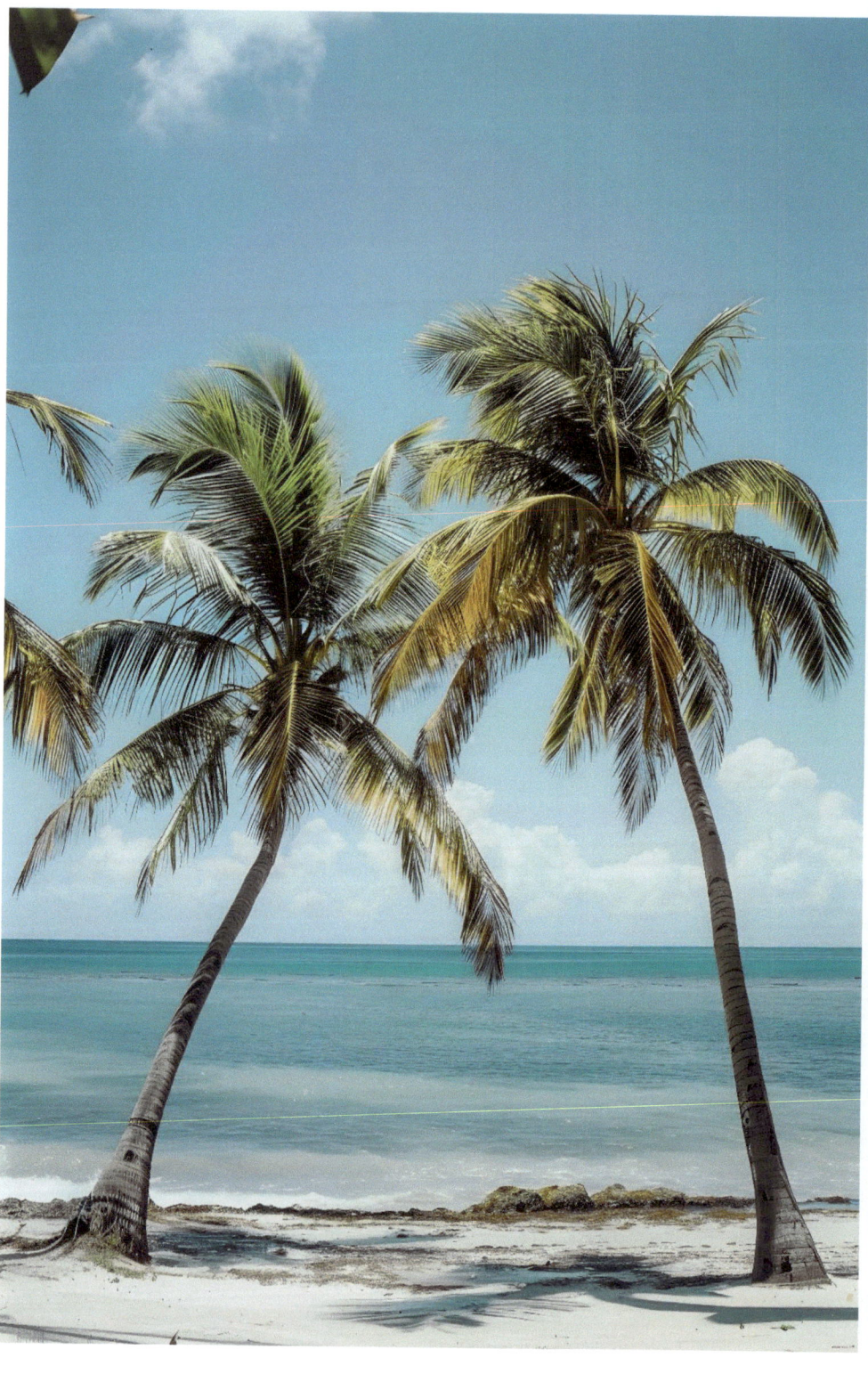

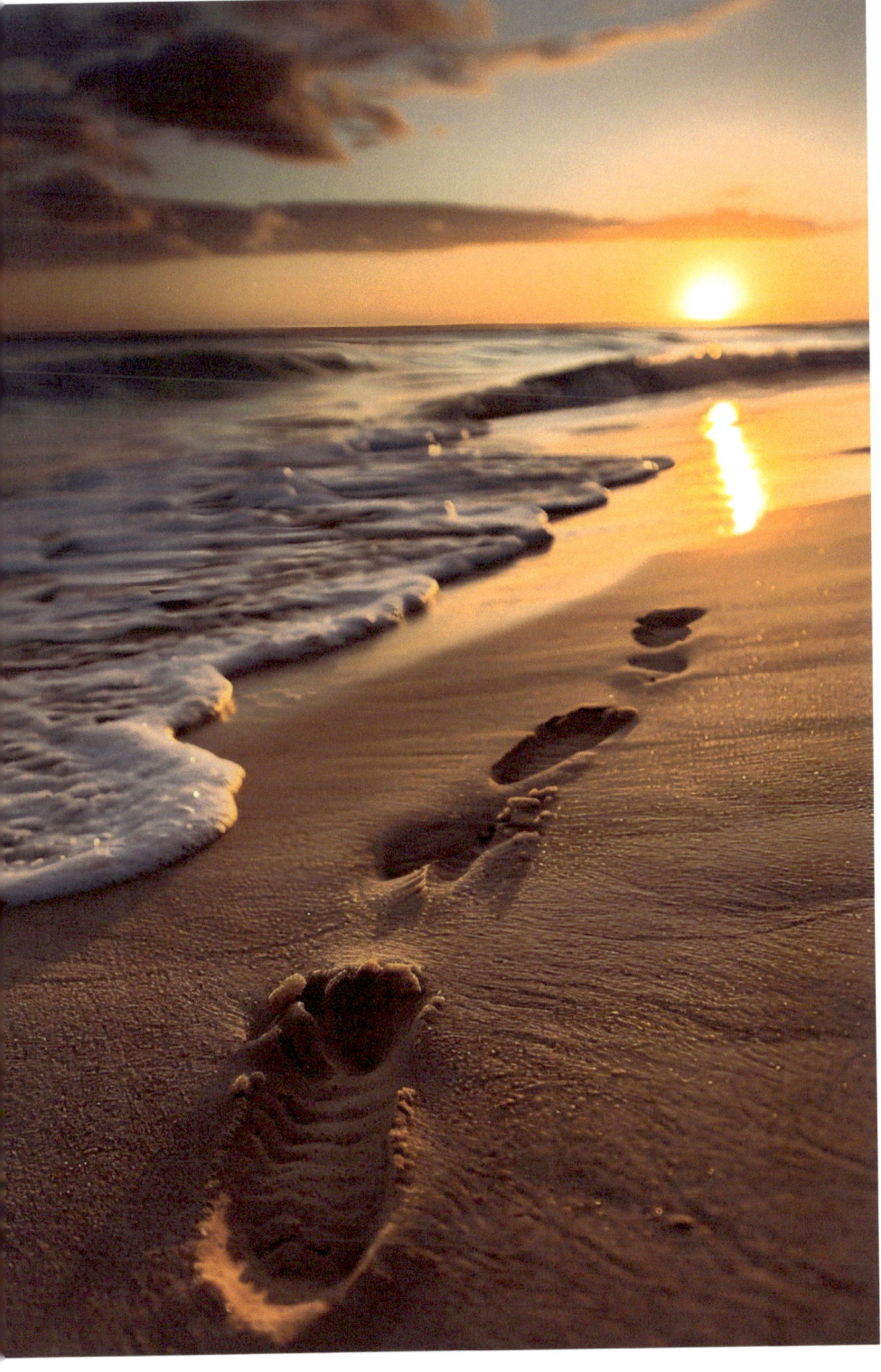

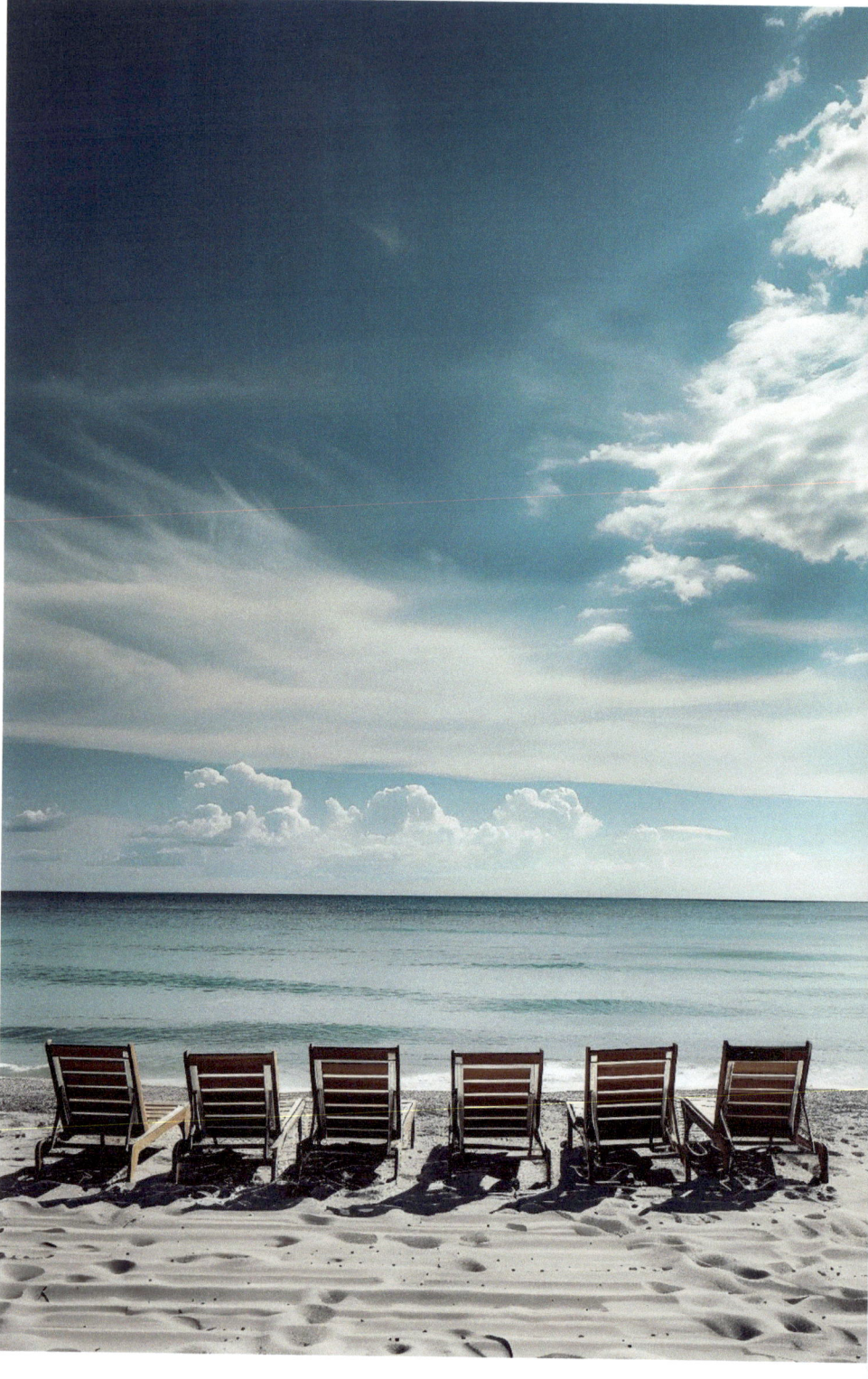

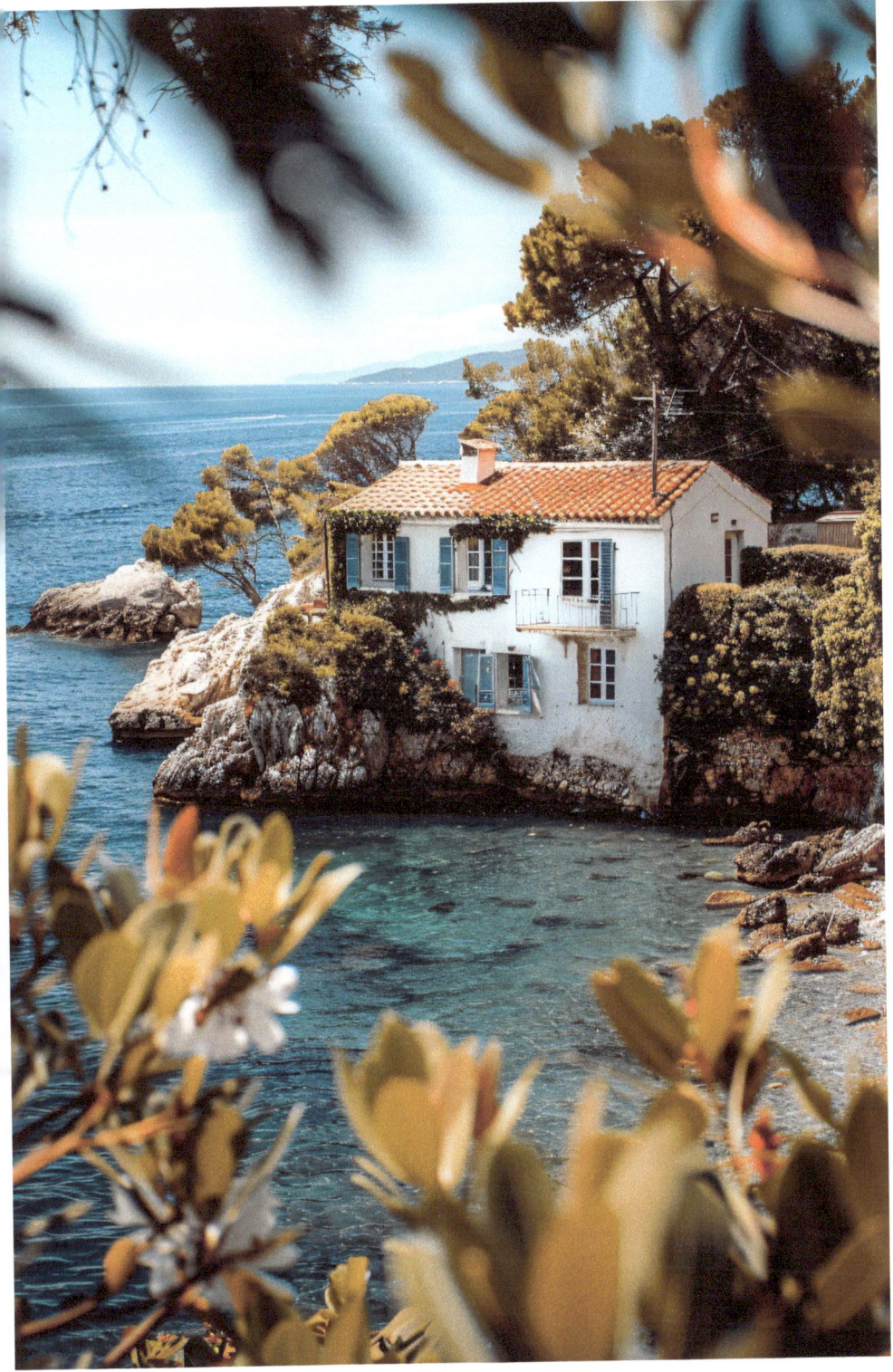

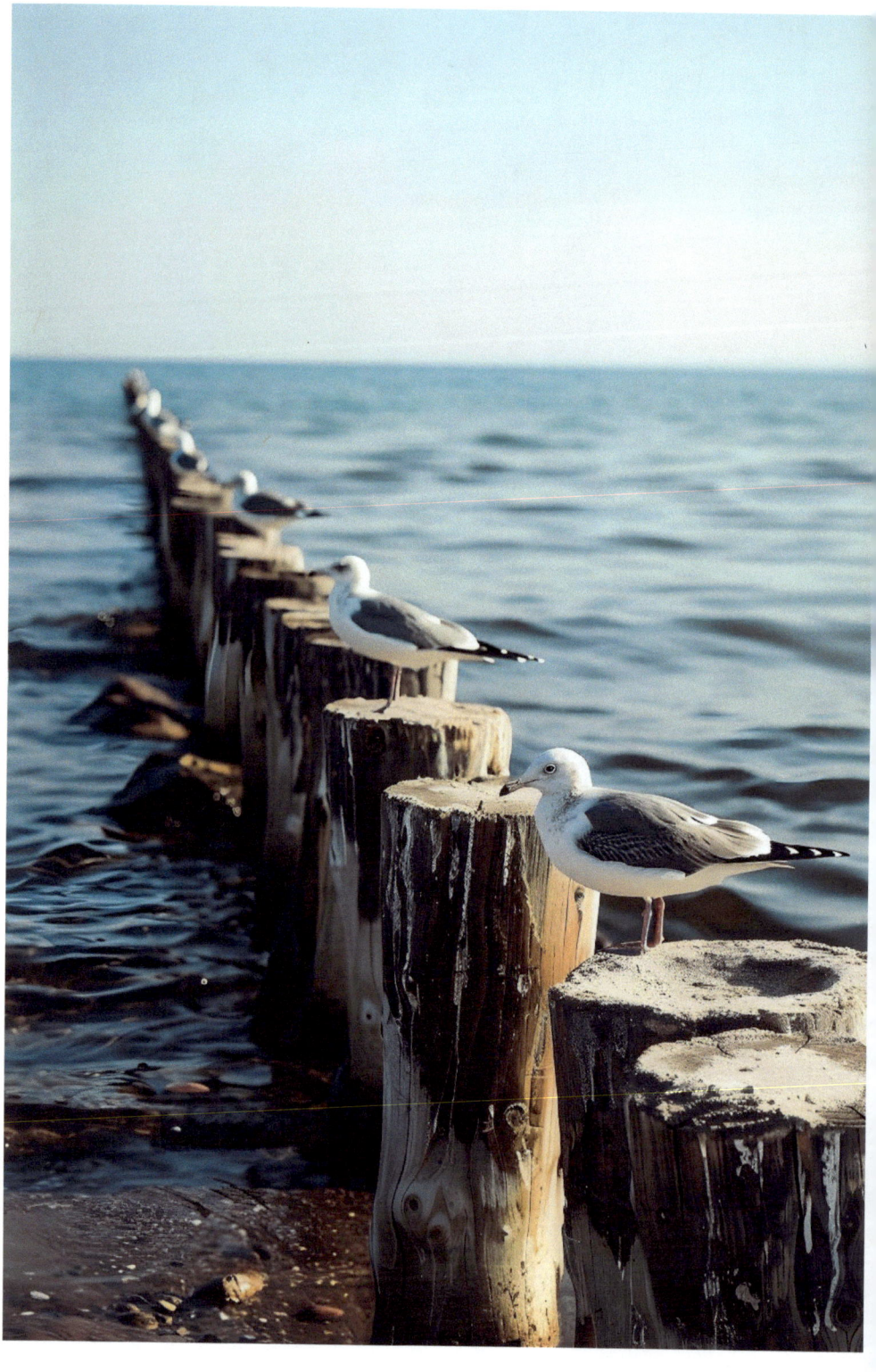

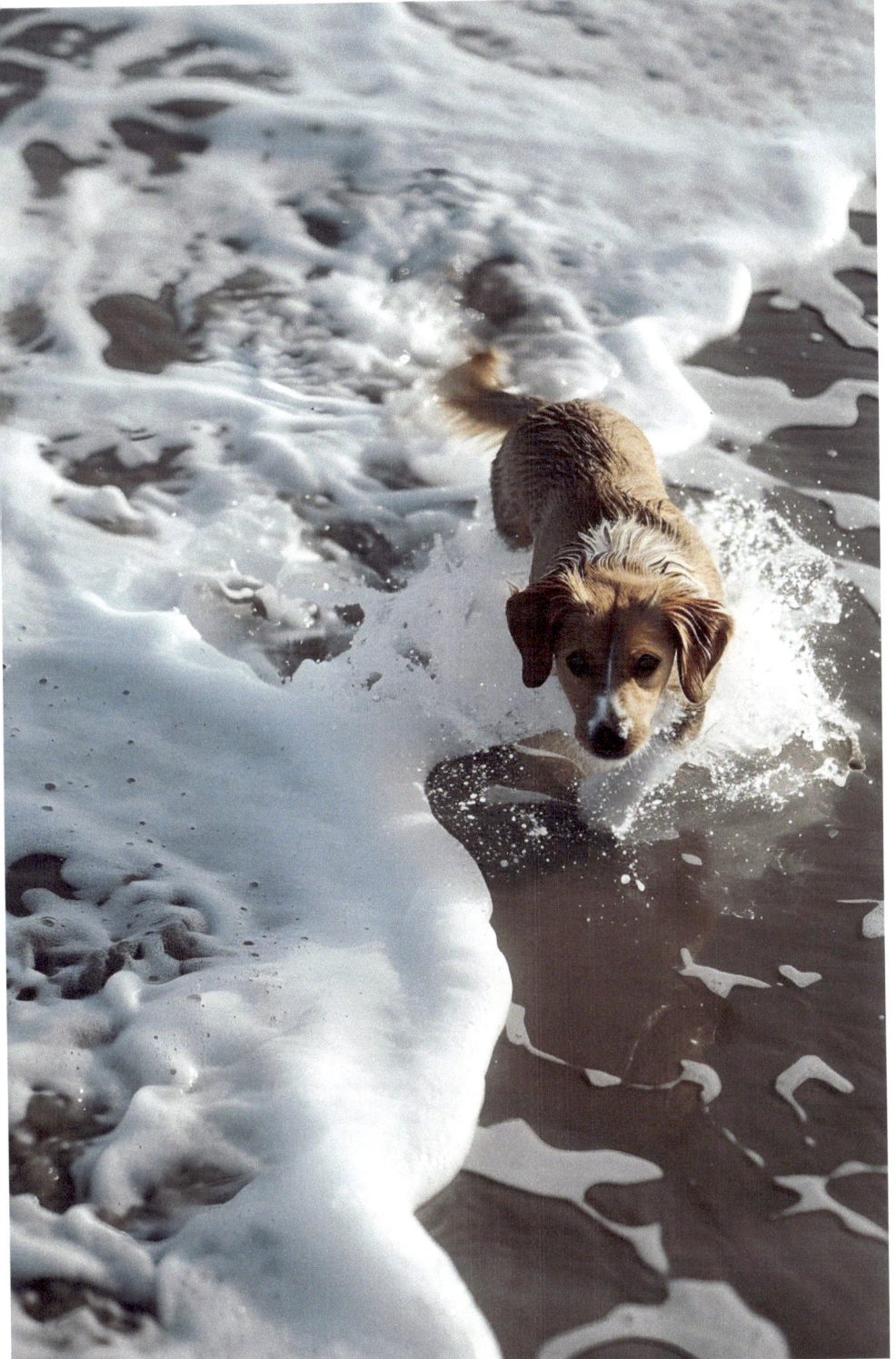

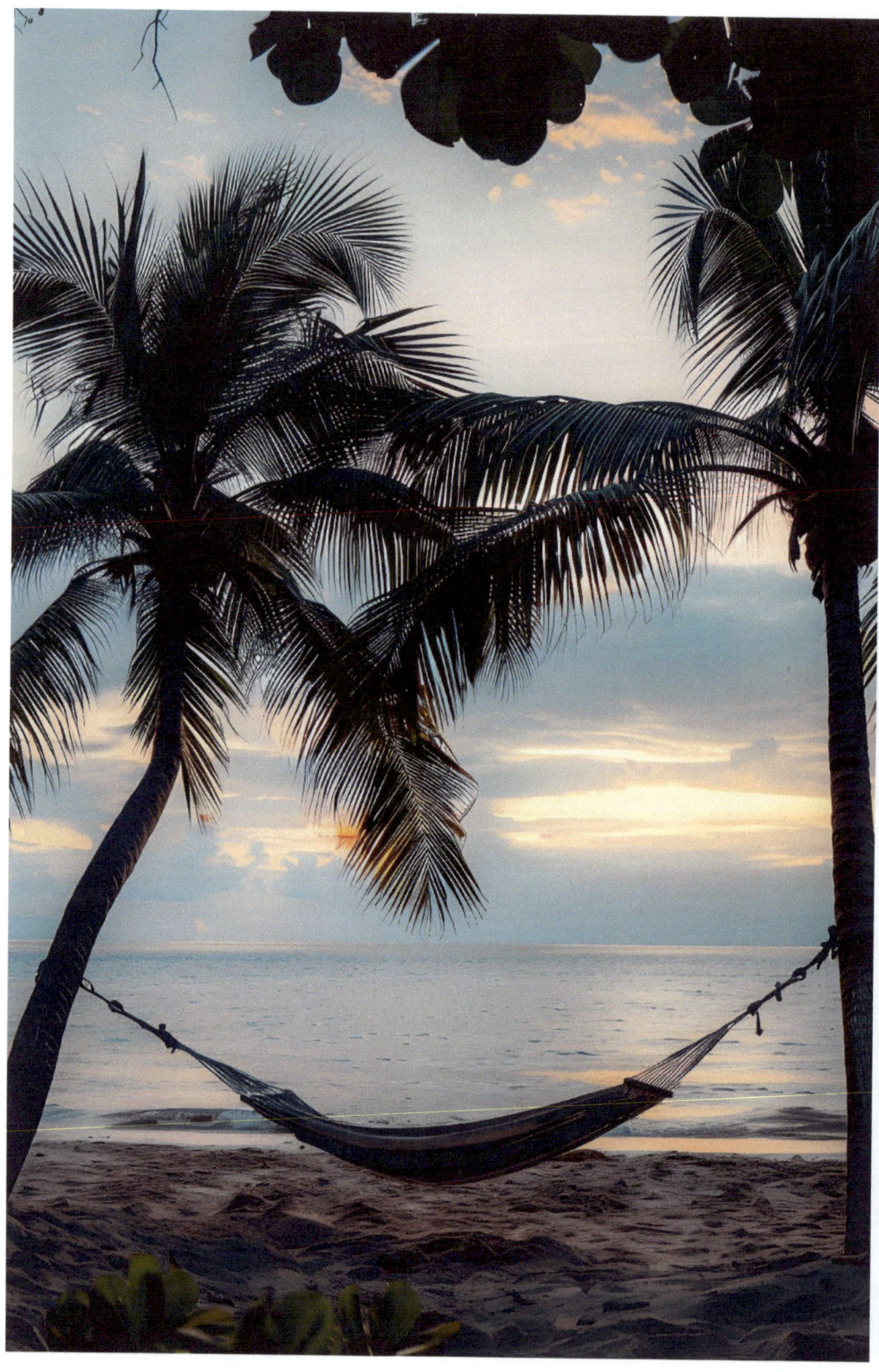

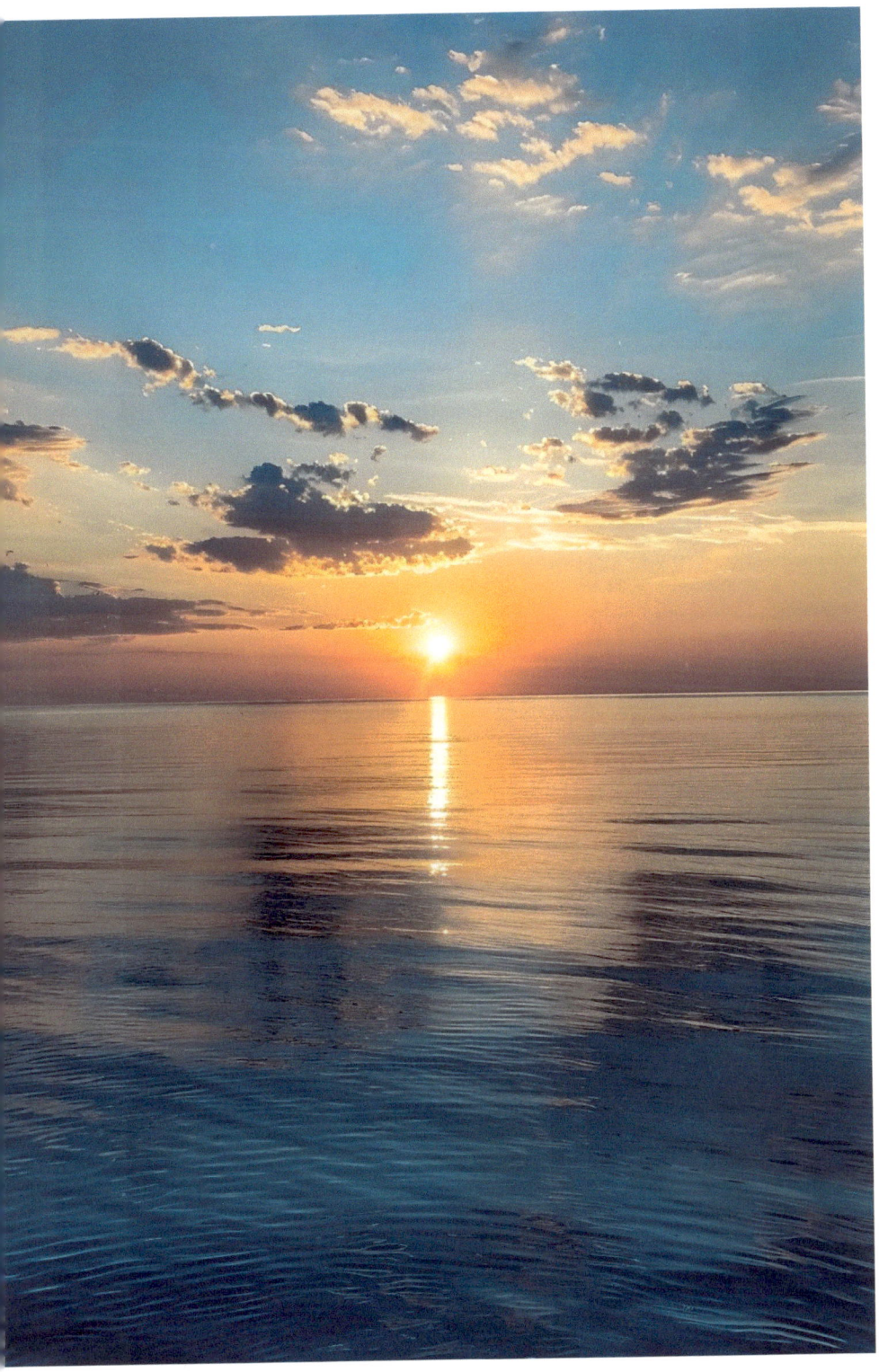

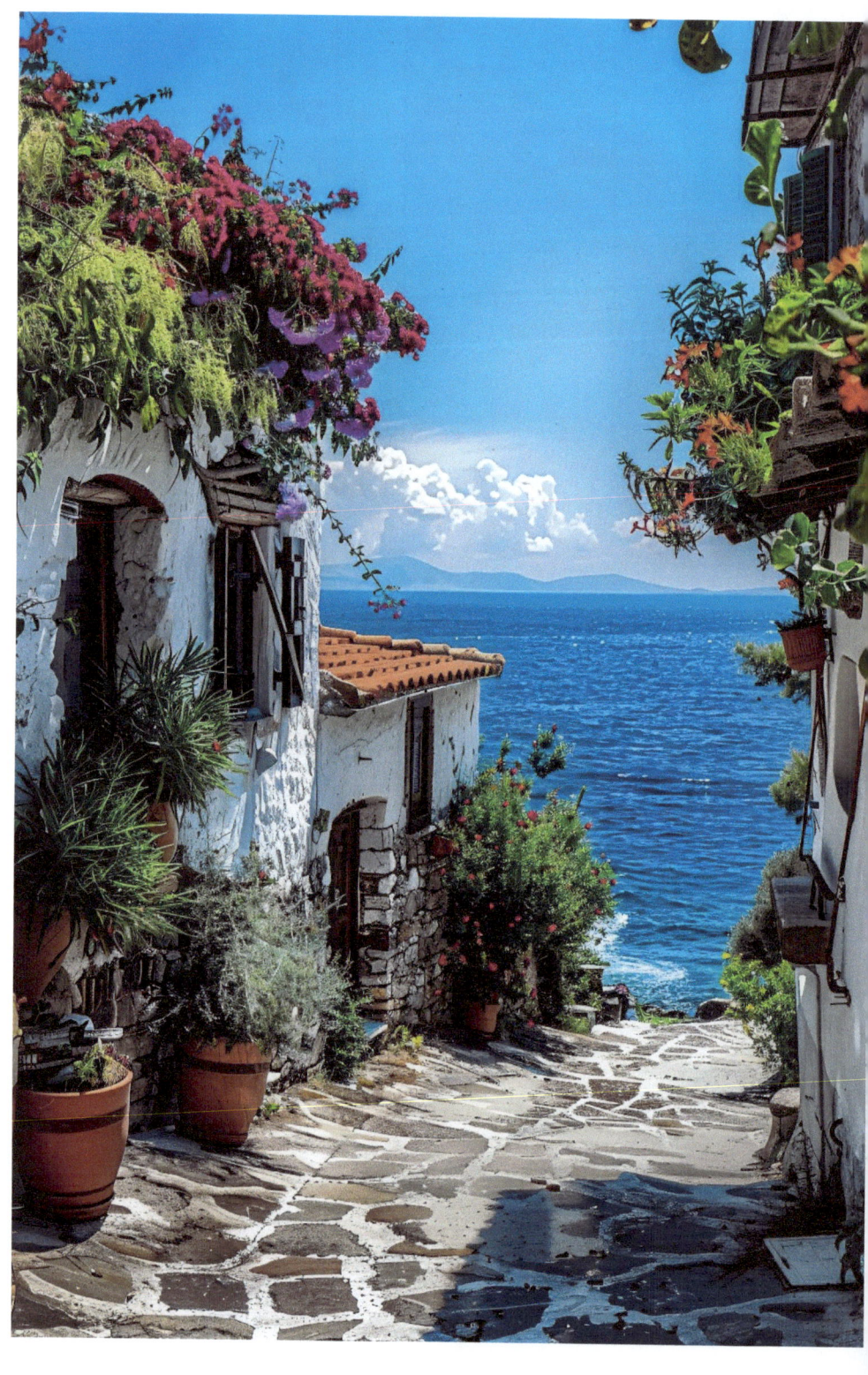

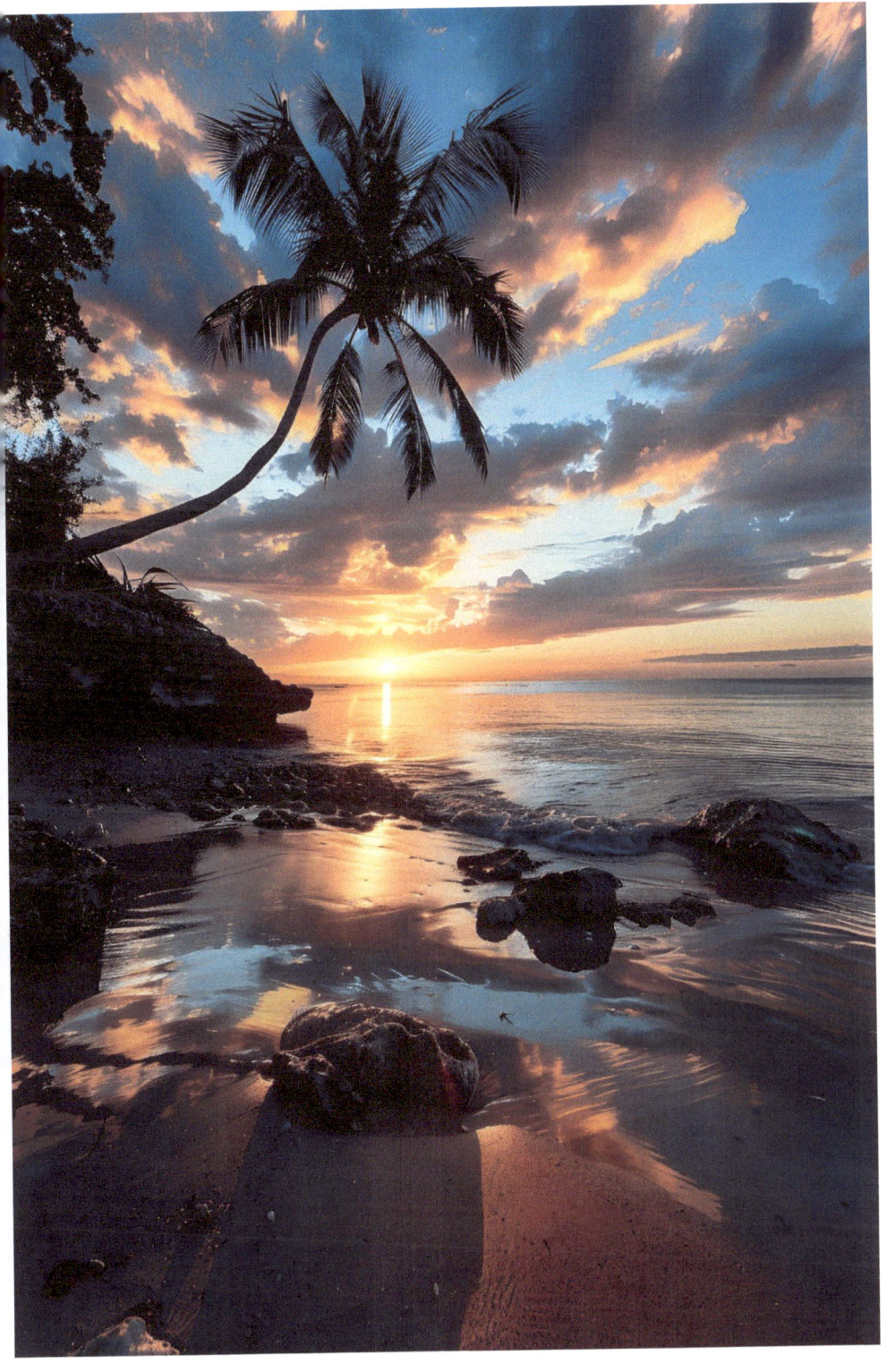

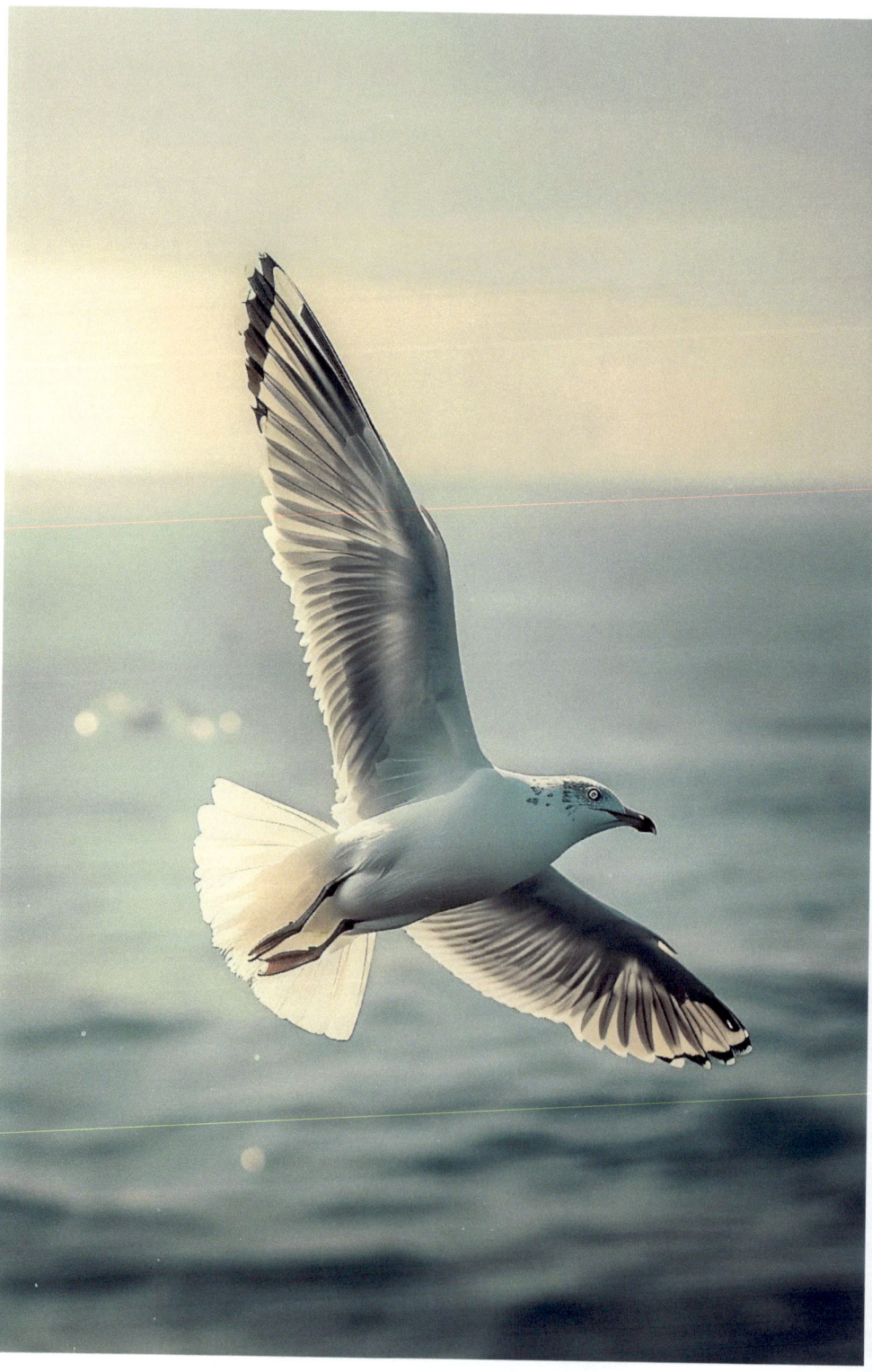

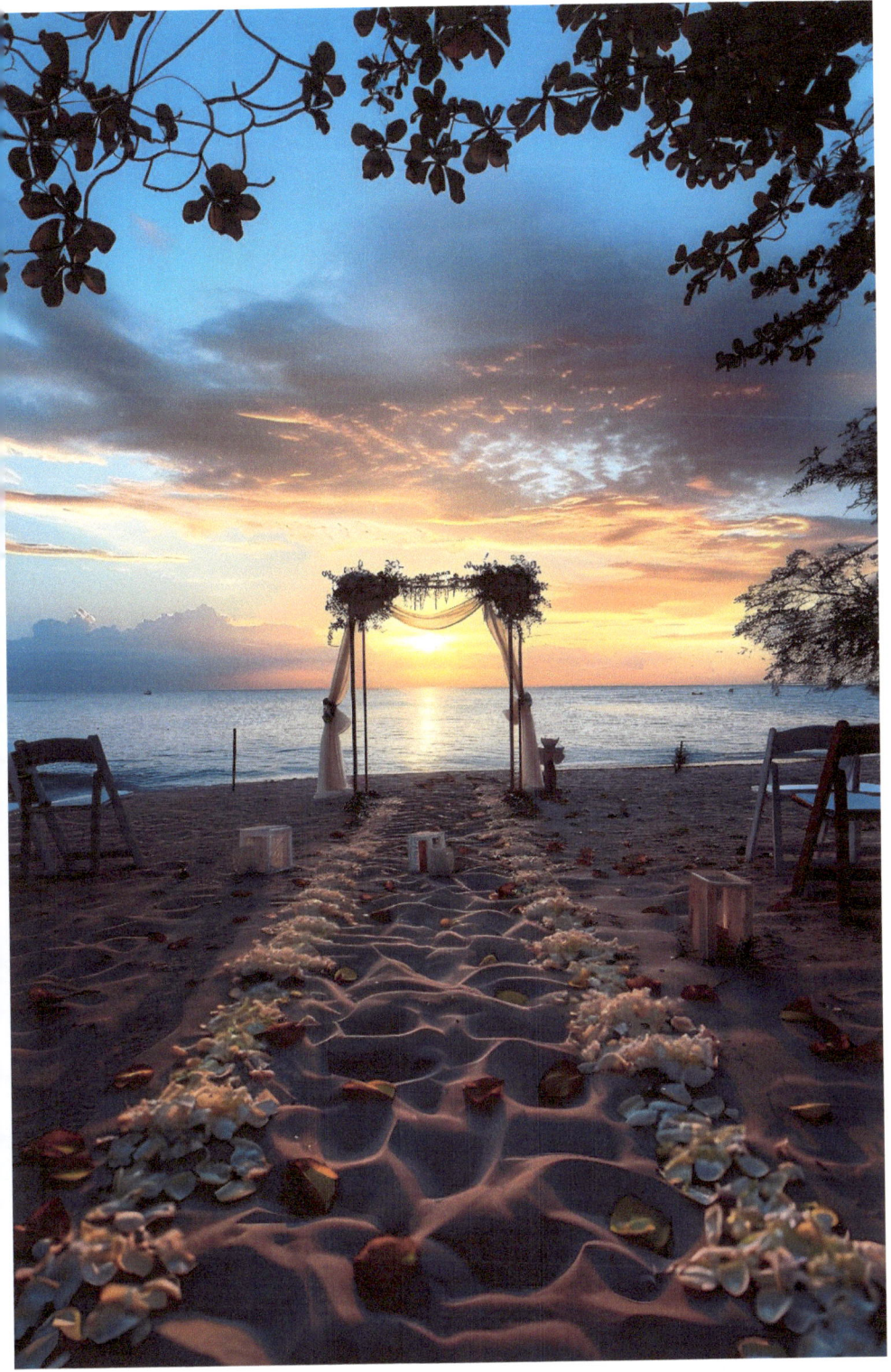

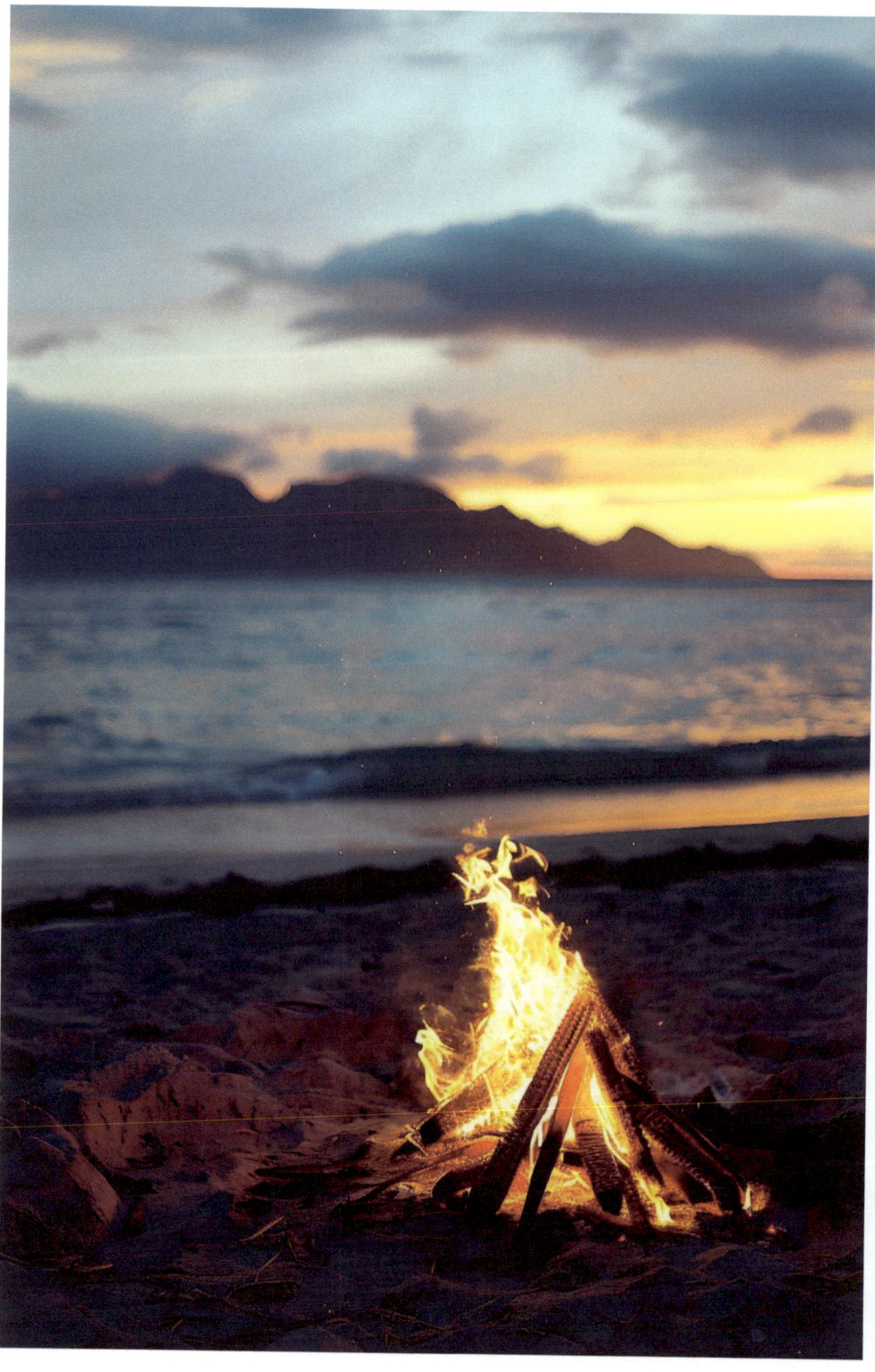

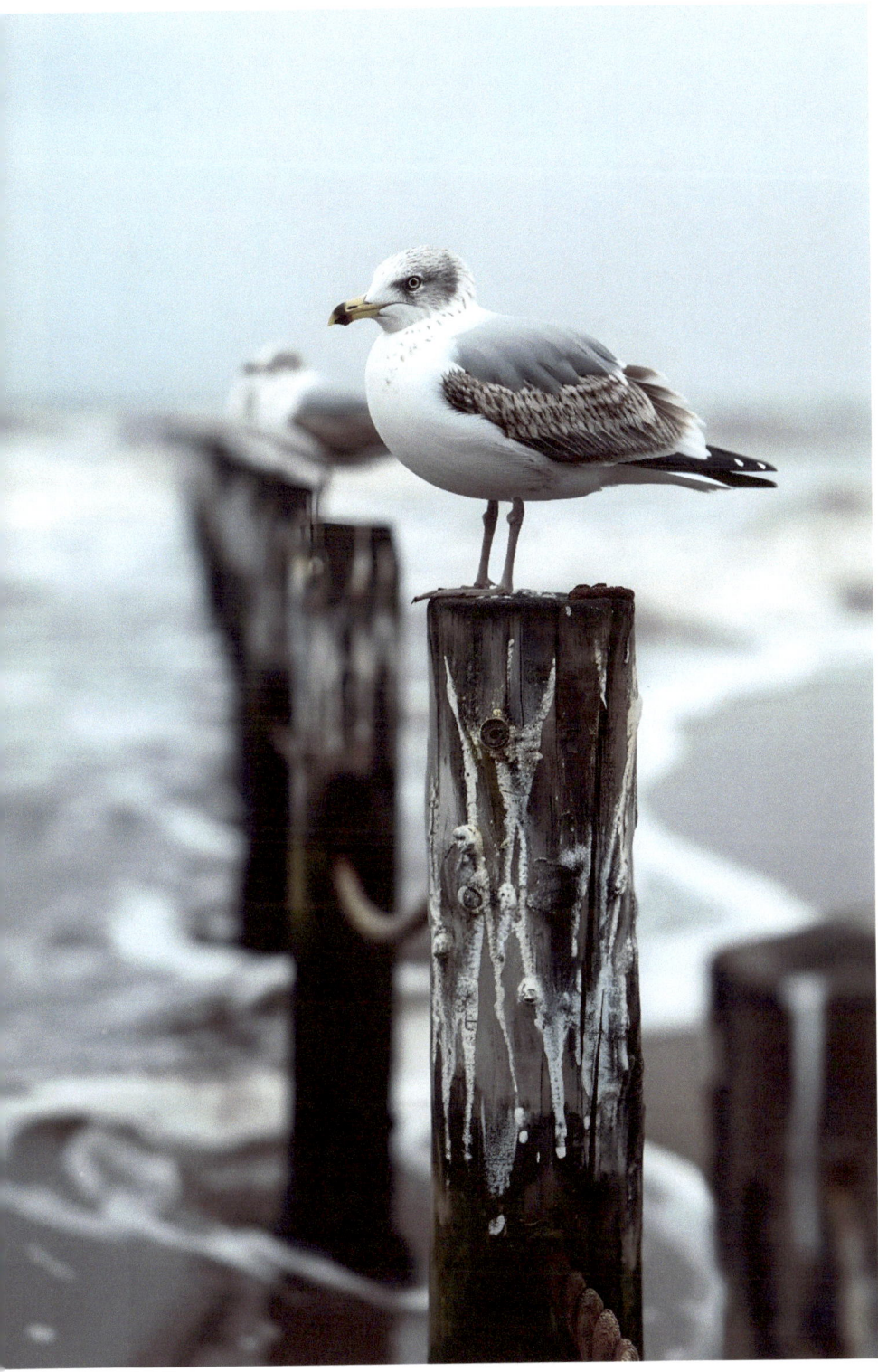

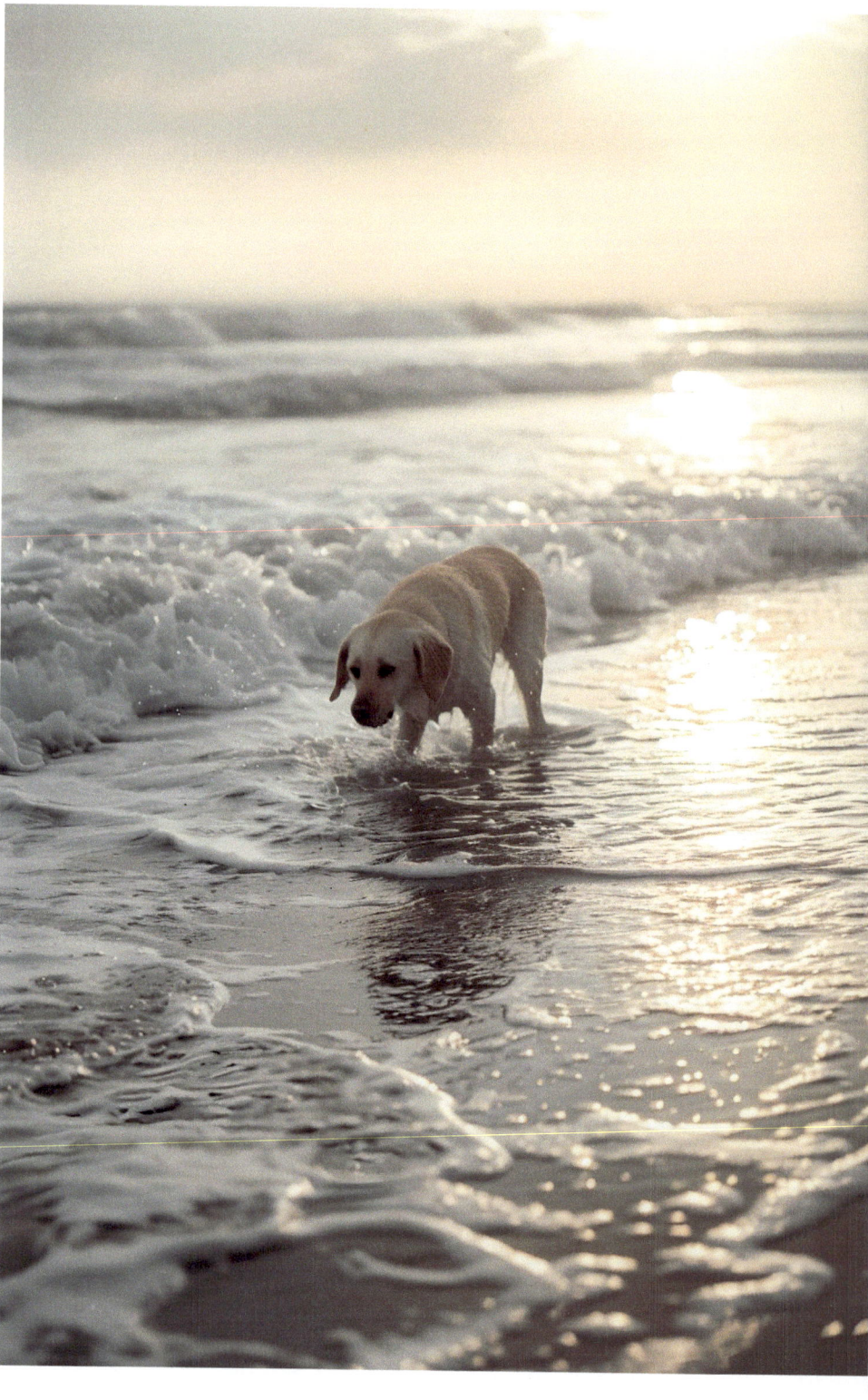

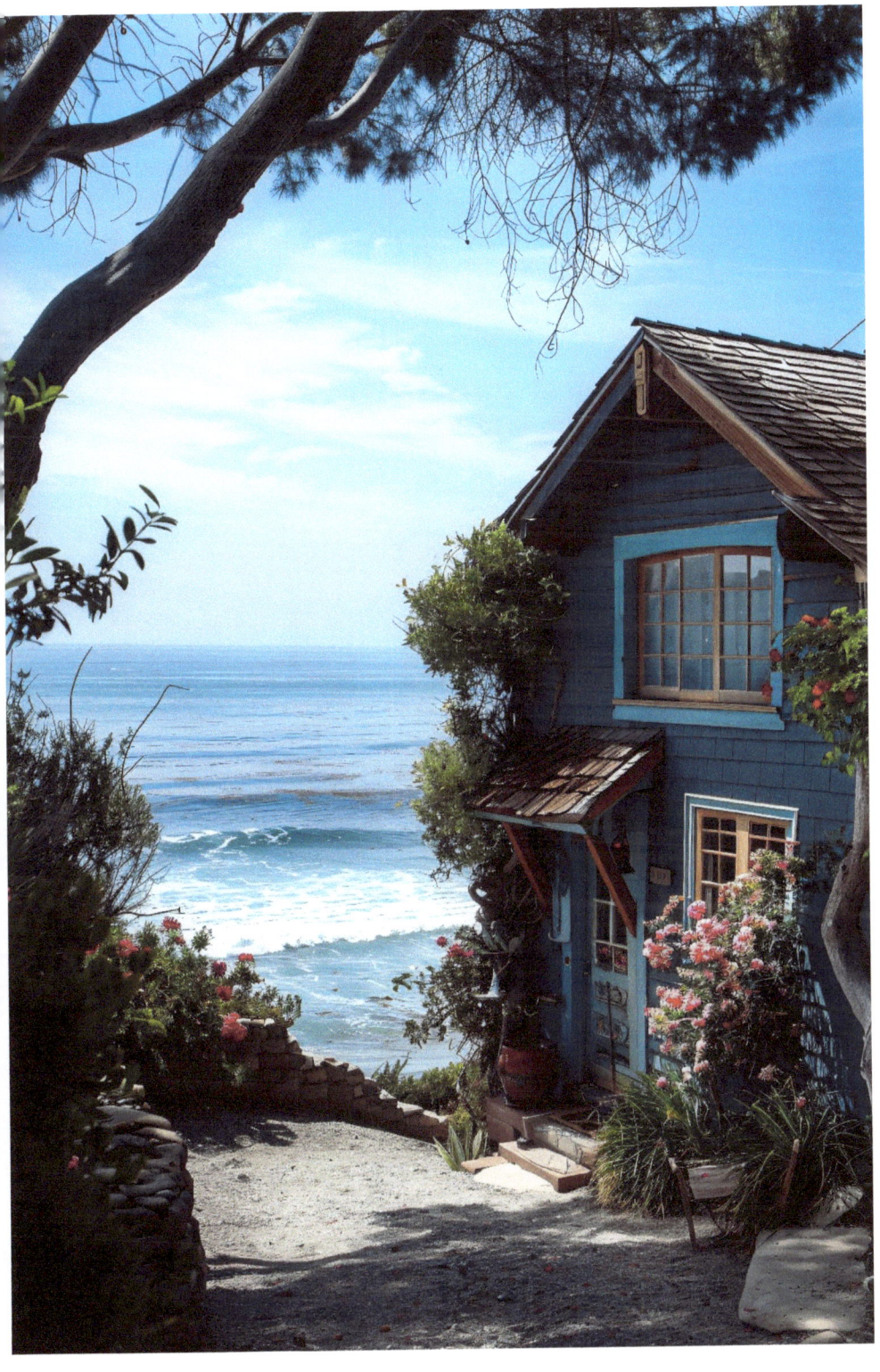

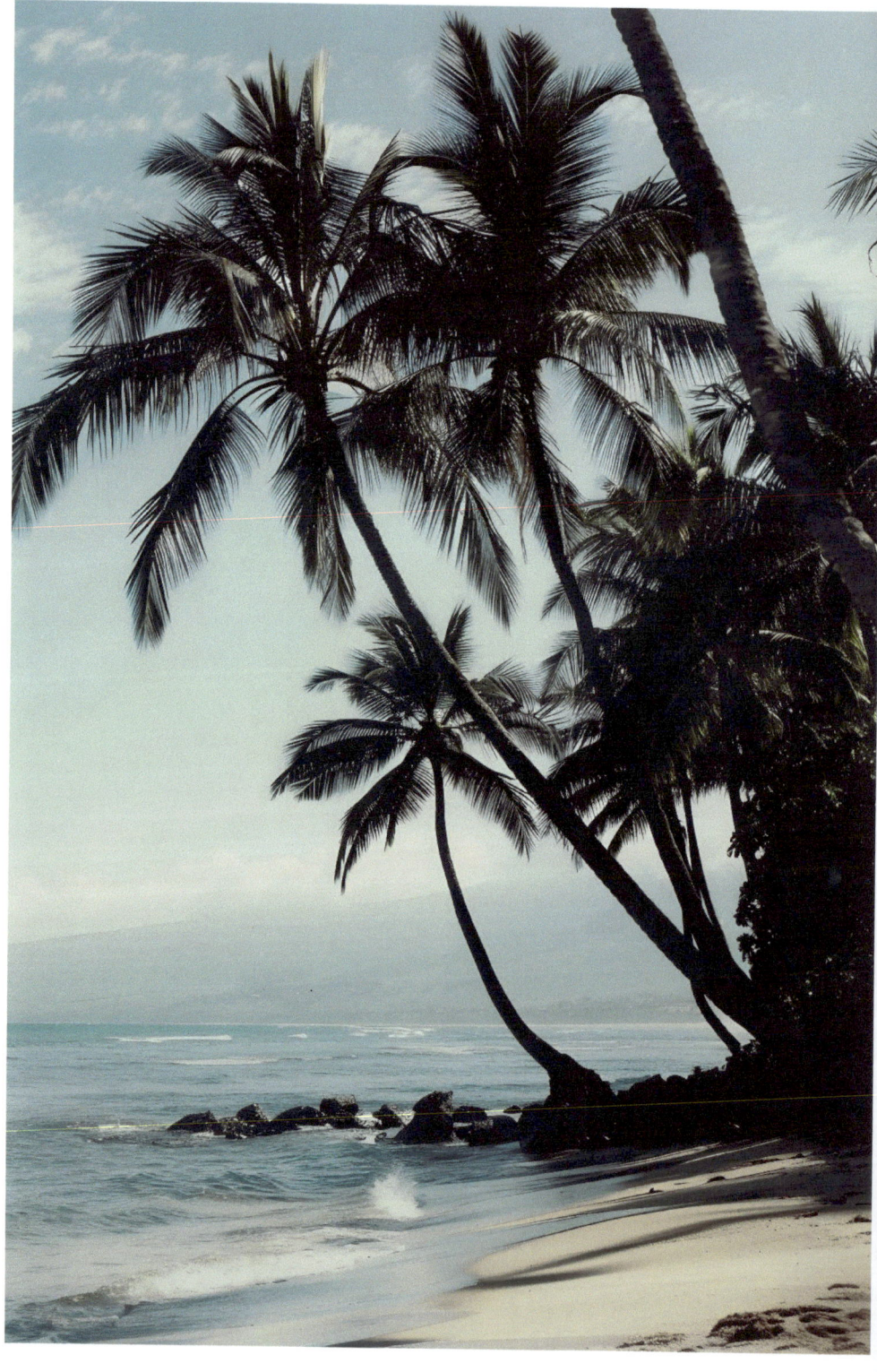

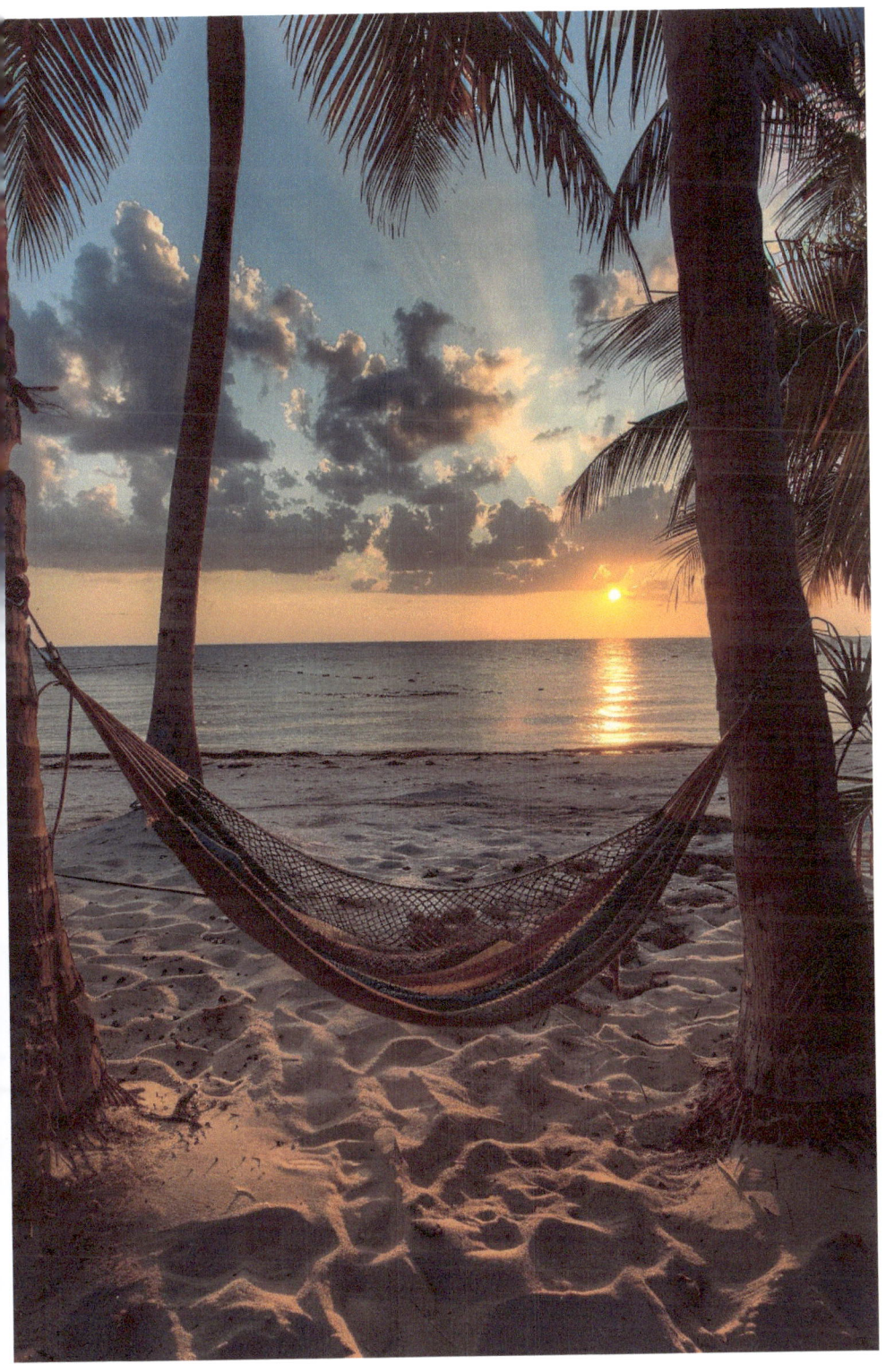

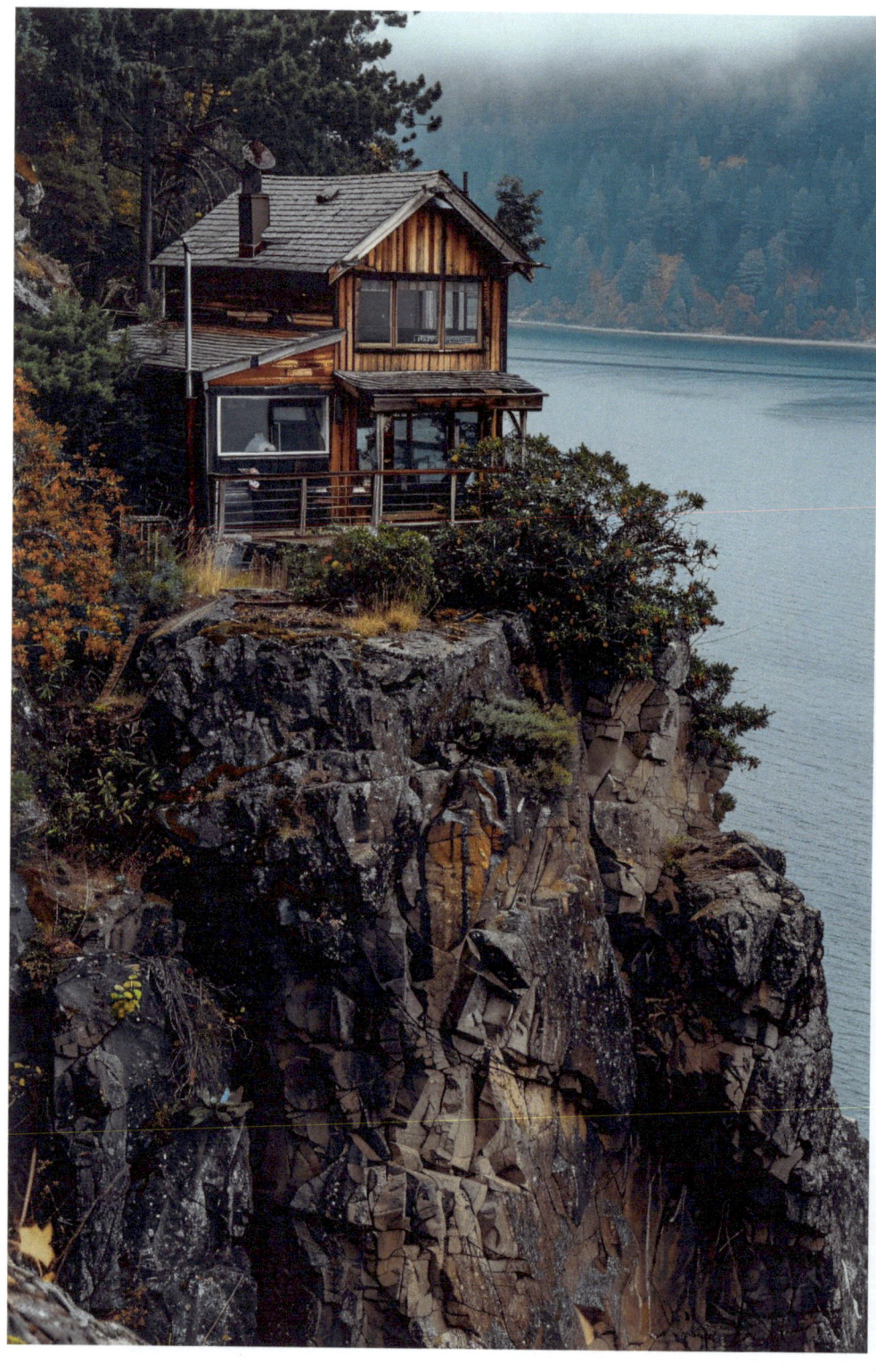

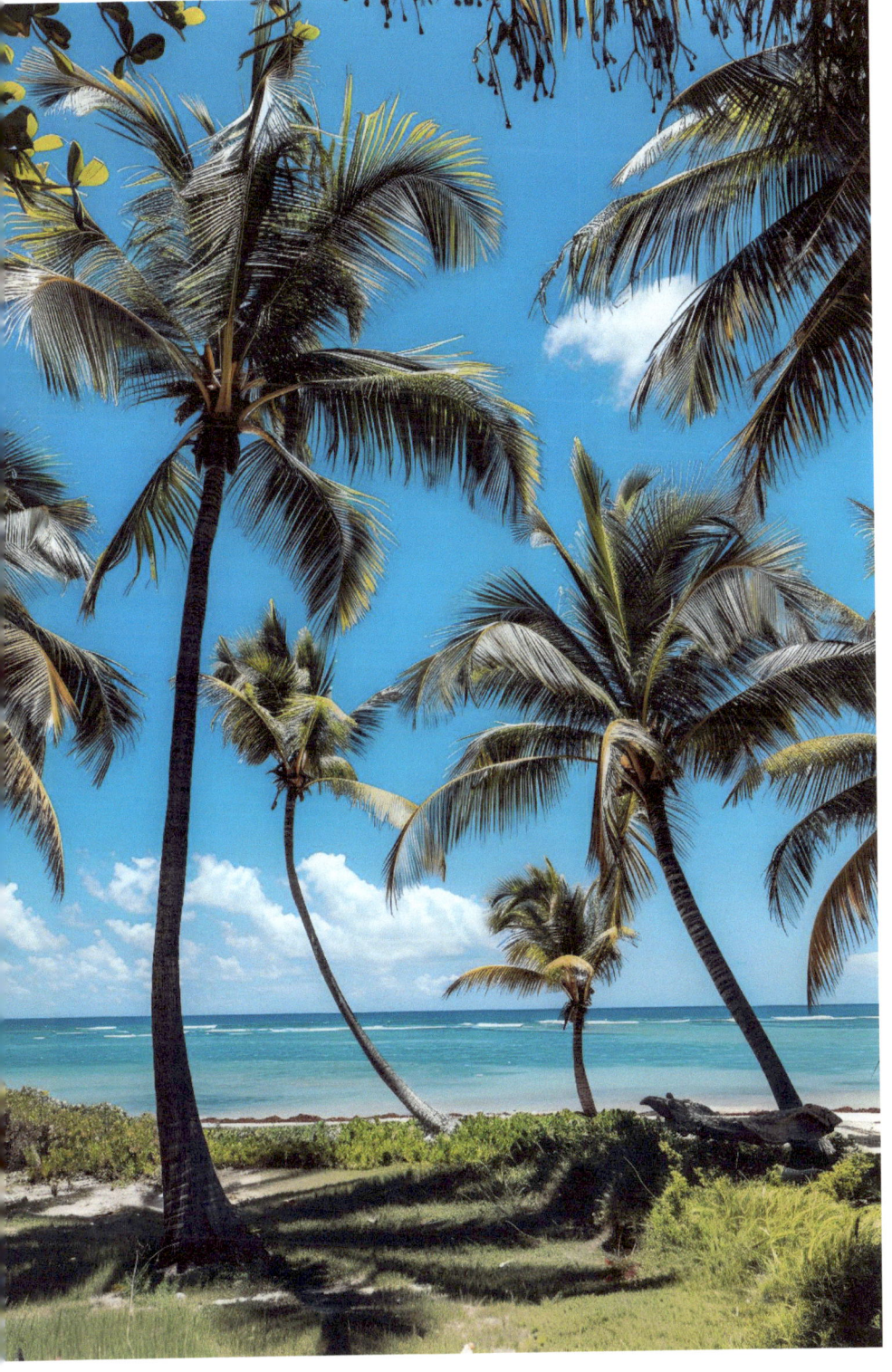

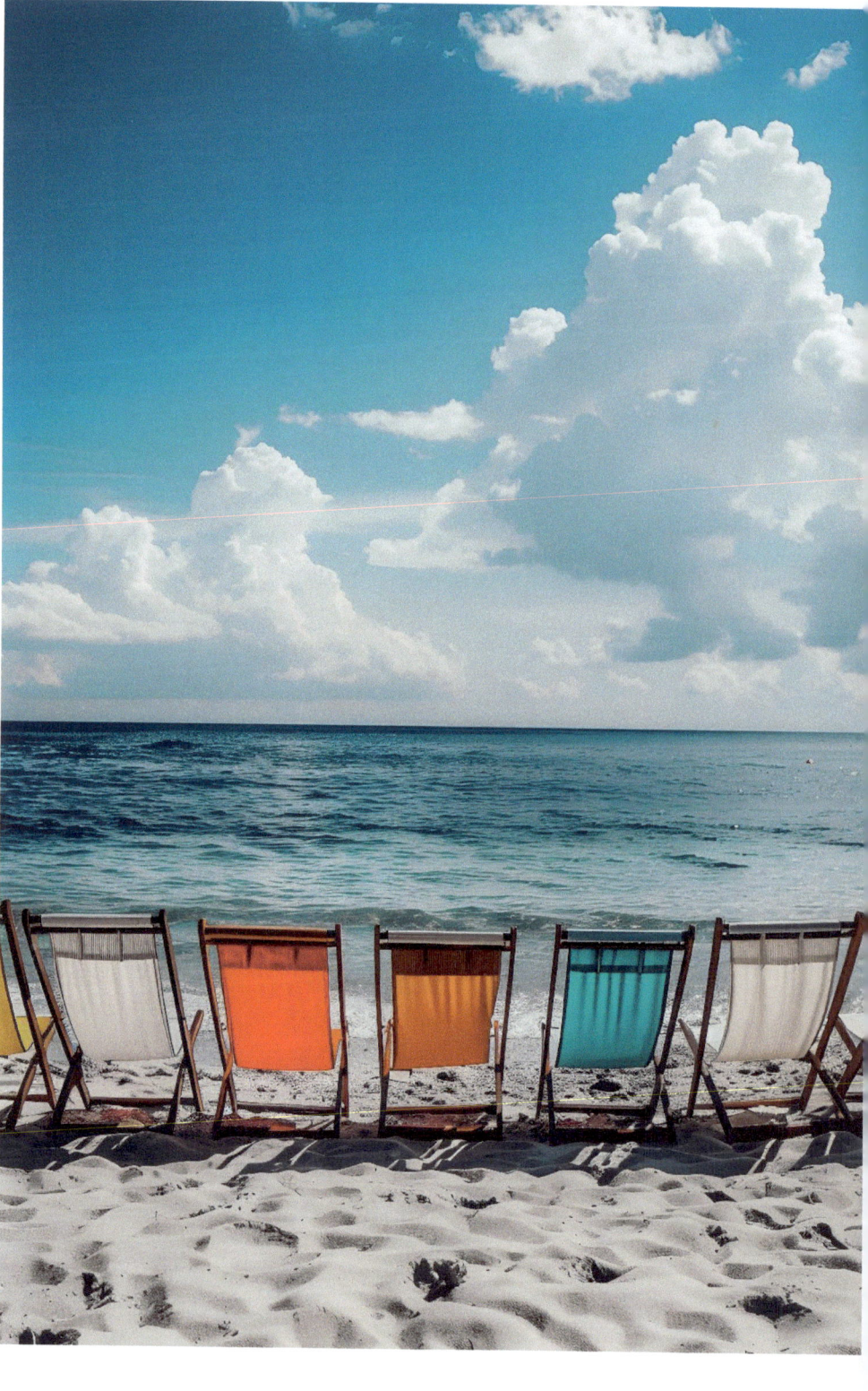

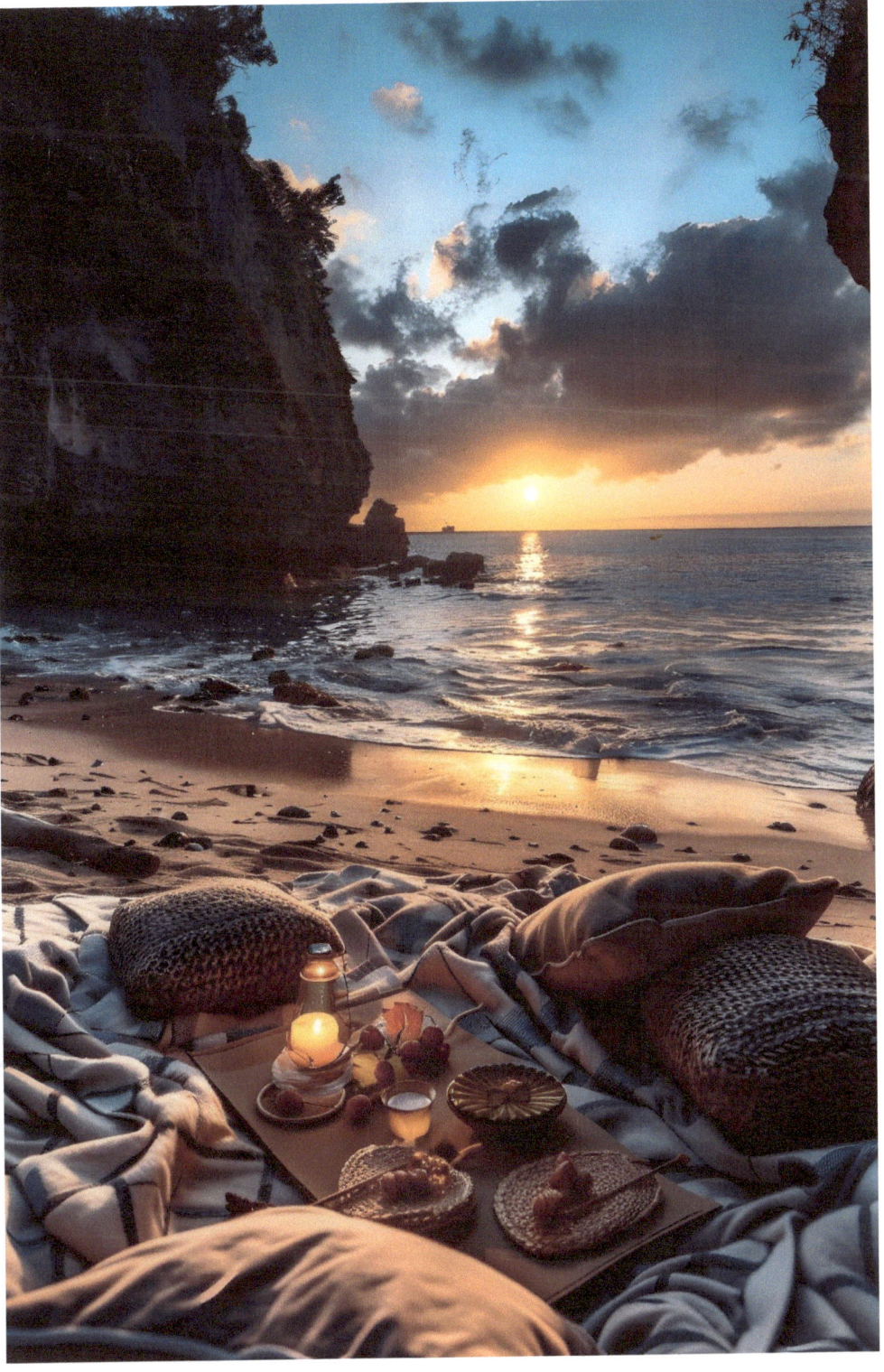

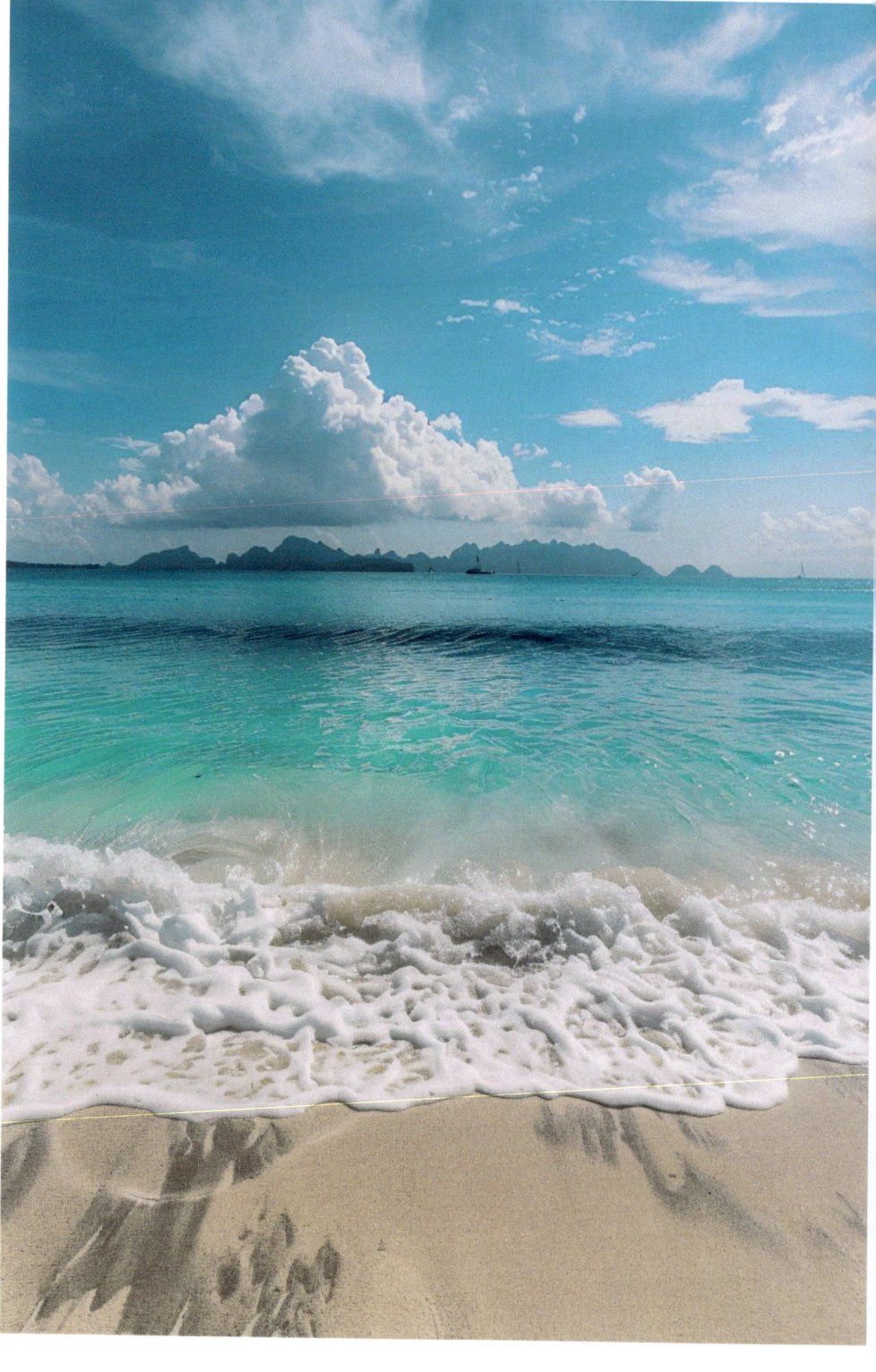

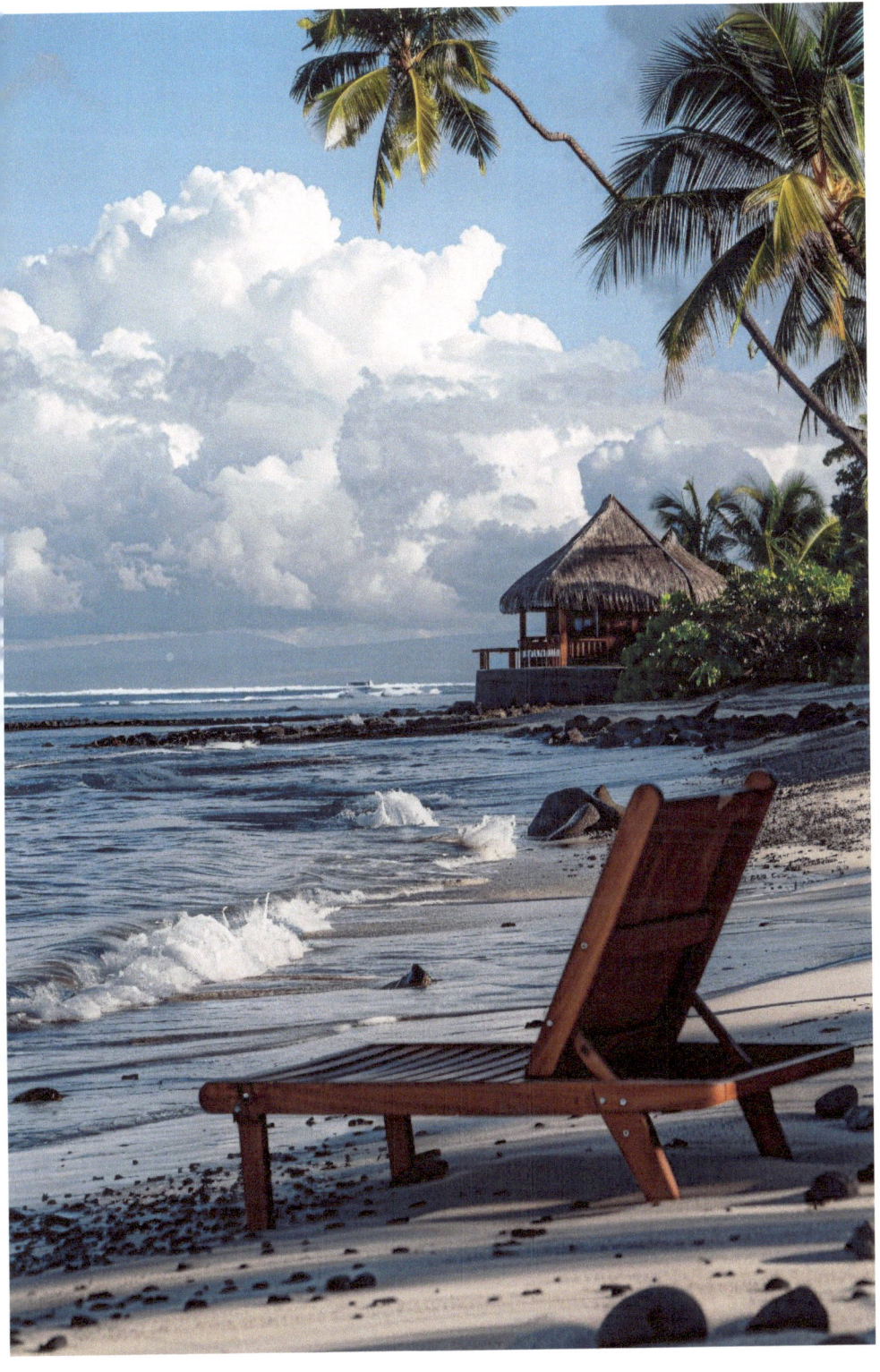

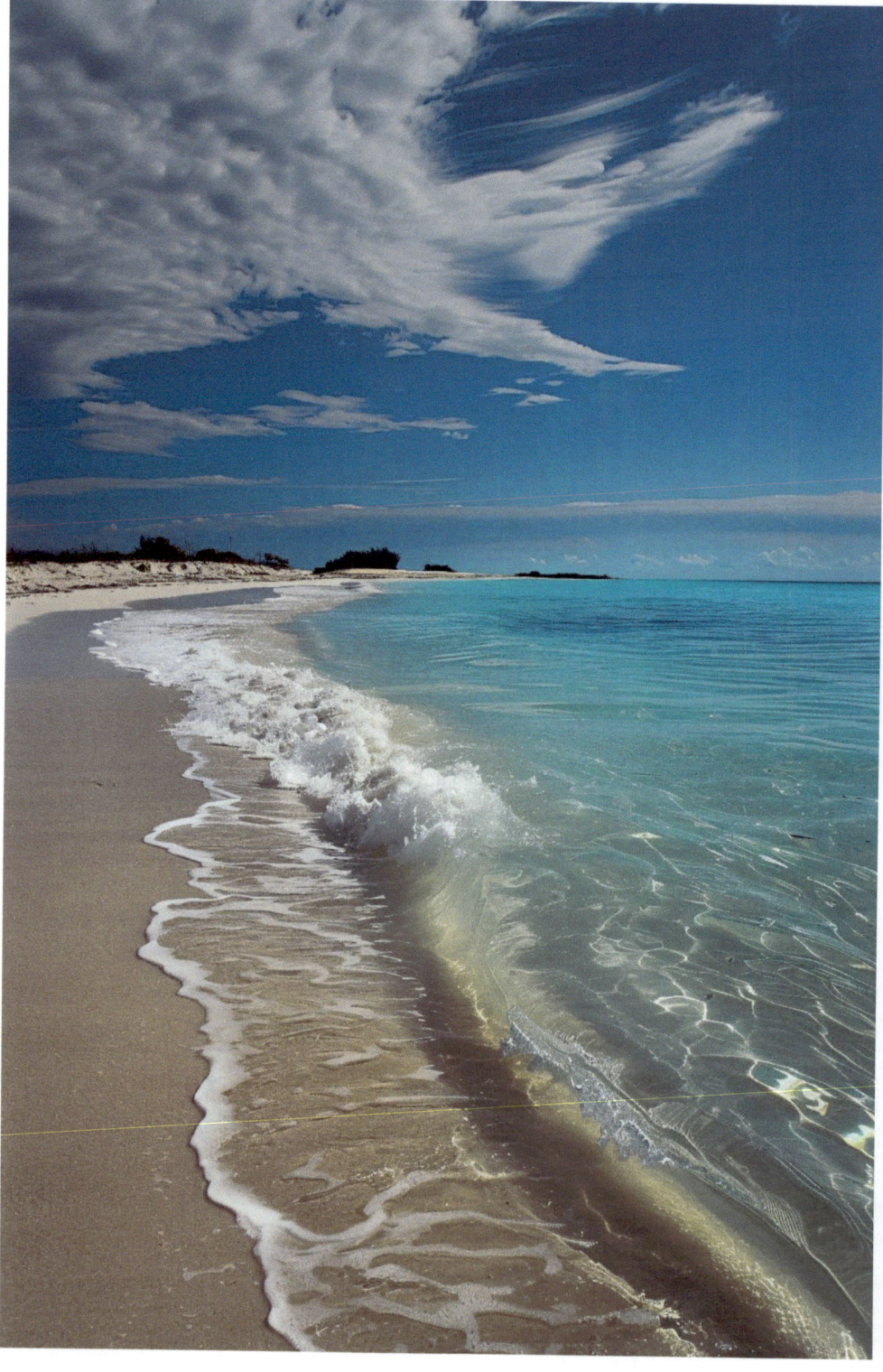

www.ingramcontent.com/pod-product-compliance
Lightning Source LLC
Chambersburg PA
CBHW040759240526
45474CB00008B/118